D1440716

International Admissions

How to Get Accepted to U.S. Colleges

MANDEE HELLER ADLER
AND AIMEE HELLER
WITH CHEREE HELLER LIEBOWITZ

FIRST EDITION

BIOGRAPHICAL PUBLISHING COMPANY
PROSPECT, CONNECTICUT

International Admissions
How to Get Accepted to U.S. Colleges
First Edition

PUBLISHED BY:
Biographical Publishing Company
95 Sycamore Drive
Prospect, CT 06712-1493
Phone: 203-758-3661
Fax: 253-793-2618
e-mail: biopub@aol.com

First Printing 2017
PRINTED IN THE UNITED STATES OF AMERICA

Publisher's Cataloging-in-Publication Data
Adler, Mandee Heller; Heller, Aimee; Liebowitz, Cheree Heller
International Admissions: How to Get Accepted to U.S. Colleges/ by
Mandee Heller Adler, Aimee Heller, and Cheree Heller Liebowitz .-- 1st ed.
p. cm.
ISBN 0997602848
13 Digit ISBN 9780997602845
1. Title. 2. International college guides. 3. Ivy League schools. 4. College entrance. 5. Career guidance. 6. Higher education.
BISAC CODES:
      STU010000 STUDY AIDS / College Guides
      STU009000 STUDY AIDS / College Entrance
      EDU031000 EDUCATION / Counseling / Career Guidance
Dewey Decimal Classification: 378 Higher Education
Library of Congress Control Number: 2017934360

Contents

Prologue

Our company, International College Counselors, has been in business for close to fifteen years. The company began as one person in a tiny home office, and now boasts five offices throughout South Florida, along with representatives in other countries. The company's secret has been to hire the best counselors in the business, and to use our collective wisdom to support our students.

Looking back, our team has worked with wonderful students from over 30 countries who have gained acceptance to colleges including Harvard, MIT, Stanford, Penn, Princeton, and Yale. Last season, we worked with one student who was accepted to seven of the eight Ivy League schools, four students with four Ivy acceptances, two students accepted to the highly rigorous Brown PLME program, one Penn Huntsman Scholar, one NYU MLK Scholar, and nineteen students who received full merit scholarships to college. We differentiate ourselves due to our commitment to our students, and to supporting their unique interests and goals.

Over the years, we have seen certain repeat challenges faced by students trying to come to the United States for college from countries abroad. At its most basic, the application process for international students often has quite a few more pieces. In addition to the SAT or ACT, all students from a non-English speaking country must take the TOEFL or IELTS, an additional test of their ability to use the English language. Then, there are items such as translated transcripts and bank letters, which the American students do not need to worry about.

Most importantly, however, is the fact that most international students do not have counselors at their schools to guide their process. And, since most students are likely to attend college in their home country, for international applicants there is often no one to push them along and encourage their focus. Hence, it is quite common to see international students miss application deadlines or forget certain pieces of an application.

This book is an attempt to clarify the international admissions process so that students all over the world can more effectively gain admissions to U.S. colleges. Please know this process is not easy: not for American students, and certainly not for those of you reading this from abroad. But, this book will give you the best advantage possible for reaching your goals.

While it would be easy to complain about the overwhelming nature of the college application process, you can't change the system, but you can change your approach. Reading this book is a great start. And, of course, for hands-on support, consider an independent college counselor, such as one from International College Counselors.

Getting into the school of your dreams comes not from connections, but from understanding the admissions process and committing yourself to maximizing your academic and extracurricular opportunities. As with most things, knowledge is power.

Three sisters who all went to their first-choice college created this book. I set my heart early on the Ivy League, and I did reach my goal for both undergraduate (University of Pennsylvania) and graduate school (Harvard Business School). My older sister, who co-authored this book, attended Boston University, a top school in the country for advertising, which was her dream career. She became a copywriter, then a creative director at a major New York advertising agency, and her writing helped make this book possible. My younger sister, a nationally ranked athlete, was co-founder and captain of the University of Florida's women's water polo team and in the Honors Program. For anyone who knows water polo and academics, that's no minor achievement. She took her competitive drive to find the publisher for this project and to help with the editing. It was a family affair, as have been all my greatest achievements to date.

Of course, the three of us alone is are only part of the story: To Jason Adler, Rebecca Adler, Sara Pearl Adler, Beverly Buxbaum Heller, David Heller, Penelope Rose Heller, Barry Liebowitz, David Liebowitz, and Matthew Liebowitz, we love you!

6

And, to our International College Counselors family, our success is due to our team approach and to your brilliant minds and committed hearts: Barry Liebowitz, Beth Barteletti, Pablo Botero, Lourdes Martinez Cowgill, Jessica Fishbein Freeman, Beverly Heller, Nicole Jobson, Lindsey Maharaj, Kerri Brewster Medina, Brenda Rudman, Jonathan Saltzburg, Julie Simons, and Justine Visan.

Mandee Heller Adler

IMPORTANT NOTES
FOR INTERNATIONAL STUDENTS

Throughout this book we interchange the words "High School" and "Secondary School." In either case, we are referring to the last levels of school you will attend before going to college.

Chapter 1

Admissions Overview: What Colleges Look For

WHAT COLLEGE ADMISSIONS OFFICERS WANT

"Pick me!" "Pick me!" your application says to a college.

But, what exactly are colleges looking for?

Colleges have many students to consider, especially since they're getting more and more applications each year. More students are looking to attend college, and applications like the Common Application and Coalition Application have made it much easier for students to apply to more schools.

Back when I was younger, you needed to fill out each college application separately. By hand. In pen. Or align it perfectly into a typewriter. You would type the essay on a typewriter. If you made a mistake, you would type it all over again. And you would write and type a whole new essay for each school. But now, it is all different.

For college admissions officers, the Common Application, and other applications like it, mean they have more applications and more work to do. Naturally, like all people, they look to make the work easier for themselves.

Admissions officers have made it easier to choose which students to admit by coming up with easy ways to cut applicants. Did you try to beat the system? Cut. Did you plagiarize your essay? Cut. Did you embarrass yourself greatly on social media? Cut. Did you try to make high school easier on yourself by taking easy classes? Cut. Cut. Cut.

Then, they have a formula of sorts to cut more students. Keep in mind that each school is different. This is a generic guideline.

9

THE ADMISSIONS HIERARCHY

Strength of Curriculum, aka High School Courses: Supreme Importance

The majority of admissions officers consistently place the greatest weight on the strength of a student's high school curriculum in the decision-making process. Colleges notice whether you took the most rigorous classes available to you or whether you opted for an easier route.

Detailed information on choosing the right courses can be found in chapter 8.

Grades in the Challenging Courses: Supreme Importance Runner-Up

Colleges prefer that you take challenging courses. It's better to challenge yourself and risk getting a bad grade than to go for an easy top grade. However, don't take a class that will bring your grades down. If you take a very hard class, like Advanced Placement (AP) Calculus and get a less than good grade, it may not be as good as a top grade in a slightly easier class. Slightly easier does not mean very easy.

I recommend that you take high school classes one level above your comfort level.

Standardized Test Scores: High Importance

SAT scores and ACT scores usually rank third. The SAT scores are often judged in "score bands," especially when combined with a top transcript. For example, an Ivy League school may consider a combined mathematics and critical reading score of 1500–1600 a "score band." If you score below 1500, you are in a different category, but anywhere within the 1500–1600 score band is considered a strong score. The same is true for an ACT score, where a strong score range is 34–36.

This means you shouldn't stress about getting 10 more SAT points. If you've scored well, you're done. Turn your attention to your grades instead.

However, students who want high scholarships need higher scores.

Students looking for special programs, like engineering, need to make sure their math scores are as high as possible.

Thankfully, international students do not need to take the SAT or ACT for admission into a number of schools. Some schools do not require the SAT from anyone who applies. Others will waive it for certain international students. Almost all schools recognize that access to the SAT and ACT is not available in all countries and will give full consideration to the applications without an ACT or SAT score from students in these countries.

Ivy League schools require the SAT or ACT.

For a list of schools that do not require the SAT, visit www.fairtest.org/university/optional.

TOEFL (Test of English as a Foreign Language) or International English Language Testing System (IELTS) scores are typically required for international students. The TOEFL/IELTS requirement for international applicants may be waived for certain students. These students must have achieved a certain score on the Critical Reading section of the SAT exam or the ACT Verbal section, or studied for at least four years in the United States or another country where English is an official language.

Students need to check the requirements of each school to which they apply. Schools are less likely to waive the TOEFL/IELTS test requirement for students who have attended an English-speaking school in a non-English-speaking country. There is good reason for this requirement—students who can't speak English well usually cannot keep up with the demands of the college classes and have difficulty succeeding.

Detailed information on tests for admissions can be found in chapter 7.

College Essay: High Importance for "Maybes," Medium Importance for All Others

Decent essays will not get you into school or keep you out of it, *except* if you're in the "maybe" pile. Of course, you won't know whether or not you're in the maybe pile, so I recommend you do your absolute best on the essays. Finish them over the summer so you have maximum time to get them perfect. Make sure you have a native English speaker or someone fluent in English check the essay and correct any grammar issues before it is submitted.

Detailed information on writing the college essay can be found in chapter 4.

College Fit: High Importance

Show a college you belong there and want to be there by doing your homework and sharing your knowledge in essays and interviews. If a college asks for an "optional" essay to go along with the Common App or their regular application, "optional" means "mandatory."

Detailed information on finding the right college for you can be found in chapter 14.

Extracurricular Activities: High Importance

Extracurricular activities are those activities you perform outside your normal high school curriculum. These activities may include athletics, creative arts, student government, speech and debate, internships, community service, and so much more. Colleges love students with diverse interests and goals. Keep in mind that whatever activity you participate in, colleges want to see a deep level of involvement and a true contribution to the school and community around you.

Detailed information on extracurricular activities can be found in chapter 11.

Your Demonstrated Interest: Medium Importance
Thanks to applications like the Common Application and Coalition Application, it's easier than ever to apply to multiple colleges. That's why schools are taking a closer look at your real interest in them. Ways to demonstrate interest include visiting the campus and introducing yourself to faculty and staff, meeting with admission representatives who visit your school, maintaining contact with the admissions office via social media, registering with the college at a college fair, and applying Early Decision* or Early Action. Make sure to sign in so the college knows you were there; they keep records.

Colleges understand that people with limited resources or who live abroad may find it hard to visit. A number of organizations including CollegeWeekLive offer free online college fairs. Students can "visit" online and ask any questions they may have for many top schools. Visit www.CollegeWeekLive.com. Students can also demonstrate interest by visiting school websites and signing up to receive more information.

Social media platforms being used by college admissions offices include Tumblr, Facebook, Twitter, Snapchat, and WeChat.

Detailed information on college fairs can be found in chapter 13.

*Applying Early Decision can make a meaningful difference at many schools, and should be considered by all students. See chapter 2 for more information on application deadlines.

Counselor and Teacher Recommendation: Medium Importance
A generic recommendation doesn't carry much weight for admissions officers who are looking for personalized insight on a student. Unfortunately, too, admissions offices are seeing more and more of these. I strongly recommend that you get to know your guidance counselor and one or two teachers well. Recommendations still count,

and if it comes down to you and a similar student, a recommendation or two with thoughtful comments can put you ahead.

Detailed information on recommendation letters can be found in chapter 5.

Interviews: Medium Importance

Many selective colleges offer interviews. A positive interview can help you make a good impression, but it is rarely a deciding factor in whether you get admitted. Interviews usually confirm an overall impression. Alternatively, a terrible interview can hurt your acceptance chances, especially if you're in the "maybe" pile. Interviews can be conducted over Skype or phone, so many times, students can participate in an interview even if they can't visit the school. Some schools also accept InitialView interviews. Information about the interviews can typically be found on the college's website. If you do not see the information, don't hesitate to call the admissions office and inquire about online interviews for students who live abroad.

Detailed information on interviewing can be found in chapter 6.

Senior Year: Super-High Importance for Students Applying for January Deadlines and Students on a Wait List

Colleges no longer tolerate slacking off during the senior year. In fact, some want to see "acceleration of educational difficulty." You've spent eleven years getting to where you are; don't mess up your chances in your final year!

Application Auditing: High Importance

I'm putting this near the end because it's about the things you shouldn't do rather than what you should do. Don't plagiarize. Chances are that you will get caught, thanks to technology. A growing number of colleges are fact-checking applications. Colleges also might look at your Facebook profile and other online presence to see if your activities match your claims.

Responding on Time: High Importance
If a college sends you an email, respond promptly with whatever information is being requested. And use professional writing. No "GR8s" or other informal spellings.

ADDITIONAL FACTORS

Underrepresented Applicants
Schools crave diversity. This gives them advantages in the rankings and makes for a more educational atmosphere, in that students will have different peers to learn from. Gender, race, ethnicity, religion, age, geographic origin, talents, and more can make you different from the rest. Colleges also "compete" to be able to say that they have the most foreign countries represented by international students. This means that students often get bonus points for coming from a country where few or no other students at the college come from. Another desired minority group is women who are interested in engineering or the sciences. I had two top admissions officers say to me, "If you have a female interested in science, we want them to consider our school!"

Legacy Status
Children of graduates often get a preferred status in the selection process. Sometimes grandchildren, nieces and nephews, and cousins do, too. This varies from school to school, and if you're counting on this to give you the edge you need, it's worth calling the admissions office and asking them to define their legacy status. Keep in mind, relations won't make up for poor grades or test scores—unless perhaps your family's last name is on a campus building.

Special Talents
Students with exceptional talents may receive special admission consideration. A special talent may be in music, sports, writing, photography, etc. If you have a special talent, write about it in your application. Along with having the talent, you must meet basic academic standards.

Recruited Athletes

In the last thirty years, college athletics has changed into a multi-billion-dollar business. Recruiting student athletes has become strategic and competitive, especially in sports like American football, baseball, and basketball where a championship could potentially increase undergraduate applications and booster donations. Coaches will make special requests to the admissions directors for certain student athletes in a wide range of sports.

CHOOSING THE RIGHT HIGH SCHOOL CLASSES

Regardless of who you are, you must choose your high school classes carefully. While there's no 100-percent-guaranteed future college admissions formula, there are a few strong patterns for success.

Meet the high school requirements.

High schools have a list of required credits that must be taken in order to graduate. Colleges don't look favorably on students who weren't organized enough to graduate.

Take a balanced set of classes.

Typically, a student should try to take courses each year in English, science, math, the social sciences, and foreign language.

Choose a smart range of college-prep courses.

A student doesn't need to take all of the hardest classes to get into college, but course choice depends on the selectivity of the colleges a student wants to attend. Demanding and challenging honors, accelerated, AP, A-Levels, and/or International Baccalaureate (IB) courses make a student more desirable to a school. However, colleges recognize a student can only take advantage of accelerated courses if their high school provides them. If AP courses or International Baccalaureate programs are not offered at a high school, colleges understand and only expect that a student will excel in the opportunities to which there is access. Colleges also understand that different schools/different countries/different curriculums have

16

different requirements that may restrict what courses a student can take. Consider taking online classes if your school is limited in course selection.

For more information on course selection see chapter 8.

Show colleges a positive pattern.
Colleges like to see a high level (or an improving degree) of rigor and success throughout a student's high school years. This includes the senior year. You've likely heard this famous question: "Is it better to take a course where I know I can get a top grade, or should I take a harder course and risk getting a lower grade?" The answer is: "It's best to get a top grade in a harder course." Students need to seek challenge, not avoid it, and succeed in the challenges chosen.

Know the admissions guidelines for top-choice colleges.
Many colleges, especially the selective ones, have specific admissions requirements for entering students—for example, a certain number of years of math courses. It is best to research each school individually. Make sure you meet any and all minimum requirements.

Pursue intellectual interests.
In secondary school, it is acceptable to take courses of a personal interest, like filmmaking or fashion; just make sure it is not at the expense of your schedule's overall rigor. Honesty is very important when deciding between different courses. Are you choosing drama because you have a real excitement about it and the challenge it presents, or are you taking the class to avoid a different (and perhaps more difficult) academic subject?

Consult with teachers, a secondary school counselor, and/or a college advisor on what courses are most appropriate for your situation.
Some difficult decisions may also need to be made about which courses to take and how to balance schoolwork and extracurricular activities.

Chapter 2

Overview of the Application Process

Take a deep breath.

The college application is hard.

But, it's hard for a reason. The colleges are testing you. They want to know if you have what it takes to go to them.

The key is not to look at the process as one giant, overwhelming whole, but as a series of bite-sized pieces.

GETTING STARTED

Keep pertinent information easily accessible.
Print out the following and put it in an expandable folder. Then don't lose track of the folder.

- Family information—your parents' or guardians' legal names, addresses, occupations, employers, colleges they attended, years they graduated, and degrees they hold.

- Your secondary school's information—address, your date of entry to the school, and your guidance counselor's full name and contact information.

- Scores on standardized tests, such as SAT, ACT, CLEP, SAT Subject Tests, AP tests, and/or other national exams.

- Scores on the TOEFL (Test of English as a Foreign Language) or IELTS (International English Language Testing System).

- High school transcript, diploma, or academic record—some schools require students to self-report all of their secondary school courses and grades, including their current courses.

- Credit card information to pay the application fee and to send the test scores.

Other information that you may need includes:

▶ Certified English translations of all transcripts and academic records and letters of recommendation.

▶ Statement or certification of finances—some schools require students send this in with their application. Others request this information once the student has been admitted.

Track all dates and deadlines on a calendar.
You can do this on an old-fashioned wall/desk calendar or program the dates into your phone and set it up to alert you as the deadlines approach.

Keep a folder for each college of interest to you.
This will help ensure that you keep all the printed materials, notes, correspondence, passwords, and photos together. They will all start running together otherwise. Whenever you send an email to a school or interviewer, or receive a response, make sure you print it out and add it to the folder. You will also want to take screenshots of completed applications and confirmations. One of our students used a screenshot to prove his application was not late. And it worked. It's best to keep all of this together.

Break down your tasks. Set manageable goals for yourself. You won't be able to complete the application in one night or even one weekend. And if you do it all at one time, it's going to be overwhelming. Pick a date for contacting teachers, counselors, or coaches who are writing recommendations. Set your own deadlines for one or two scholarships at a time. Set a time with your parents to complete the financial aid forms. (There's a detailed description of financial aid options in chapter 19.)

INTERNATIONAL COLLEGE COUNSELORS TIP:
Send all applications in at least one month prior to the Priority Deadlines.

This way, you can confirm receipt and resend any missing documents.

Plan ahead when it comes to transcripts and recommendations. All transcripts must be official documents issued by your high school and provided in the original language. Some high schools send colleges your transcripts over the computer. Other schools make students fill out a paper form and will send the transcripts by mail. For confirmation, visit your guidance counselor's office, find out your school's way of doing things, and make the request at least two months before a deadline.

Almost all international documents required by colleges must be accompanied by official English translations if the originals are in another language. Sometimes documents in languages like Spanish or French are acceptable, but check with the college first to see what they want.

Deadlines are not flexible except in extreme situations. Students should be persistent in getting the documents they need. If you are the first student from your school to go to a U.S. college, be prepared to explain the American college admissions process to the people from whom you need letters or documents.

Send your test scores in on time.
Students must request that test scores be sent to all of their colleges by the deadline. At most schools, your application will not be considered without your scores.

Here's where to sign up for standardized tests and request your scores:
SAT score information: www.sat.collegeboard.org/scores
ACT score information:
    www.actstudent.org/scores/send/asrphone.html
TOEFL score information: www.ets.org/toefl/ibt/scores/send/
IELTS score information:
    www.ielts.org/book-a-test/getting-your-results

Send in your Financial Certification.
As an international applicant, many universities require you to certify that you have sufficient funds to cover your expenses while attending all four years at the university. Some colleges require this certification as part of the admissions process, while others require it upon acceptance, and others don't require it at all.

Universities usually accept a note or statement from your bank or financial institution as proof of sufficient funding. Many also require the student to complete and return a Financial Certification Form (FIF). Check to see whether your desired school requires this certificate, what exactly must be included, and make sure it's in on time.

AN APPLICATION OVERVIEW

The Common Application
With the Common Application, you can fill out one application and submit it to all participating schools to which you are applying.

As of the publishing of this book, the Common Application has over 500 members in 48 states and the District of Columbia, as well as in eleven countries. This number makes it the dominant electronic site for submitting applications to colleges.
> www.commonapp.org

The Universal College Application
The Universal College Application has 43 member colleges. Like the Common Application, one application can be sent to many schools.
> www.universalcollegeapp.com

The Coalition for Access, Affordability, and Success Application
The Coalition developed a free platform of online tools to streamline the college application process. More than fifty-five institutions accept the Coalition Application.
> www.coalitionforcollegeaccess.org

Common Black College Application
The EDU, Inc. Application allows you to complete one application and have it submitted to over thirty historically black colleges and universities (HBCUs) at the same time for only US $35.
www.eduinconline.com/index.html

State- and School-Specific Electronic Applications
A number of colleges and universities have their own applications that can be found on their website.

INTERNATIONAL COLLEGE COUNSELORS TIP:
Fill out the appropriate application for the school. Both the Common Application and Universal College Application websites have lists of member colleges and universities.

COLLEGE APPLICATION HINTS AND TIPS

Triple-check even the basic information.
This means your name, address, birth date, and email address. Make sure that you use your legal name and that it is spelled correctly and consistently on your applications and official documents. Misspellings and nicknames can lead colleges to think that two different people exist. Make sure you use the right abbreviation for your country. Ask someone else to look it over before you send it out, just in case you missed something.

Print-preview your application.
Do this before you hit send. Do a PDF view to make sure that your complete answer shows up. If you don't see it, neither will the admissions officers.

Write all the essays, and write them right.
Make sure you send in all the essays requested by a school and keep the essay lengths to the guidelines specified.

Submit all parts of the application.
If you are applying through the Common Application and do not submit the supplement to the schools that require it, your application is incomplete. If you forget to send official test scores, transcripts from all schools you have attended, certified translated transcripts or certification of finances (if required), and recommendation letters as required by individual schools, your application is also incomplete. Make sure everything is submitted before the deadline.

Track deadlines and submit early.
There is absolutely no reason for your application to be late. The deadlines are clearly posted on admissions office websites. Convince yourself that your application is due at least a month before the deadline. Computer servers crash and snowstorms occur, but colleges do not care. Colleges do not have to accept your application after the deadline.

Follow up.
Once you submit your application, most schools will send you a school ID and login information to check on your application status. Do this immediately and keep track of what pieces are missing. When you send missing pieces in, follow up on them too. For schools without an online confirmation system, send a simple email a week or two after you submit your complete application saying, "I want to confirm that you received my application and all supporting documents." Be sure to include your application ID with such a correspondence.

Don't assume your counselor will take care of something.
Many colleges do not send counselors alerts, so an independent counselor or high school counselor will not know if any information is missing from your application. You and you alone have the final responsibility for making sure the college or scholarship has everything it needs. (See "Follow up" above.) Colleges want to see that you are responsible enough to attend college.

Follow directions.

If a school or scholarship says it needs something by a certain deadline, send it in by the deadline. If it says an essay should be 500 words or less, make it close to 500 words or less. What the college wants, the college should get. If you are submitting your application online, the box you type your essay into may cut you off after the maximum number of words. Make sure you do not paste in your essay and send it in without double-checking to see what has been saved.

VIP APPLICATIONS: WHAT ARE THEY?

Every fall, a number of high school seniors will receive a personalized email or letter congratulating them for qualifying for a special "VIP Application." *VIP* stands for "Very Important Person." But don't get excited yet.

These applications are sent from colleges to select students encouraging them to attend the school. The VIP Applications offer a fast-track, simplified application process and often stress the offer being good for a "limited time."

Select students are typically those with high SAT scores and those who are academic high-achievers. Some schools send these applications to students who merely registered to take the SAT, live in a certain area, requested information, or visited campus.

VIP Applications also come under the names "Presidential Select," "Select Scholar," "Priority Application," and others.

Ultimately, these special applications are a marketing trick with benefits for both the school and the student. These applications help increase a school's applicant pool. For students, VIP Applications are often quick and easy to fill out. Many times the student's name and address are already filled in. Typically they don't require a long essay and applying is free.

An acceptance is not a binding commitment. It's also worth noting that receiving a VIP Application is not a guarantee that you will be accepted. If you received a VIP Application, feel flattered and complete it if you have some interest in the school. It's a good opportunity of which to take advantage. Students often get the chance to receive an early acceptance to a school, and having an early acceptance can ease anxiety. Though, if you're not a good fit for the school, you should spend your time elsewhere. You'll have more than enough to do as is.

HOW TO AVOID APPLICATION FEES AND SAVE MONEY!

In 2017, the most common college application fee charged by colleges was US $50. Stanford University charged US $90 per application, followed by Columbia University and Duke University charging US $85 per application. But there are ways to avoid the fees:

Apply to a school with no application fee.
Oregon's Reed College is one without a fee. Others have included Tulane University, Oberlin College, Lewis & Clark College, Smith College, Union College-New York, Case Western Reserve University, and Grinnell College.

Be a legacy, sibling, or family member of an alumnus.
At some schools, like Barry University, the University of Richmond, and Butler University, being a relative of an alum can get you a free application. Call and ask the school.

Visit the school.
Some schools offer an application waiver as "appreciation" for making the effort to visit. Alfred University is one. Penn State (other than the University Park campus) is another one. Schedule an appointment at the Office of Admission so they know you were there. Also find out the school's policy on application waivers in advance. Some schools require you to submit an application while you're on campus.

Call the school and ask.
Some schools offer application waivers during certain time periods of the year. Others will give you a fee waiver with an alumni recommendation. Then there are other schools that will give you a waiver simply if you ask nicely.

DEADLINES

Early Policies can maximize your chances to get into a school, but you need to read them carefully.

The names sound similar, but there are huge differences. You do not want to get caught violating school policies, so be sure to read and understand the rules for each school.

Early Decision
Binding
Students can apply Early Decision to only one college. "Binding" means that you agree to attend the college if it accepts you and offers adequate financial aid. If you're accepted via Early Decision, you must withdraw all other applications. Students who aren't accepted early, and are not rejected, are still considered with the regular applicant pool. The typical Early Decision deadline is late October to early November. If you want to compare financial aid packages, do not apply Early Decision. Early Decision applicants often have the best chances for admissions. If you really want to attend a college, be sure to consider the Early Decision option.

Early Decision II
Binding
This is similar to Early Decision, but with a later deadline. The acceptance rate for Early Decision is generally higher than it is for regular decisions regardless of whether you are in the first or second round. The typical deadline is January 1 or January 15.

Early Action
Nonbinding
Early Action is not binding, meaning students who get accepted do not have to commit. The typical deadline is late October to early November. Usually, Early Action has few restrictions and benefits the student by allowing them to hear early from a school.

Single-Choice Early Action/Restrictive Early Action
Nonbinding
You can apply early to only one school—but the decision is non-binding. See each school's website for details, as there are some differences among the restrictions. For example, in some cases you can still apply early to public colleges or to college scholarship programs.

Priority Admissions/Priority Deadline
Nonbinding
Priority admissions is just like the regular deadline. After that deadline has passed, schools accept applications on a case-by-case scenario.

Regular Decision
Nonbinding
Your application gets sent in for the regular admission pool. Most students apply for Regular Decision. The typical deadline is December 15–January 15. Students who get accepted do not have to commit.

Rolling Admissions
Nonbinding
The school reviews applications as they are completed. A number of schools, particularly big state schools, use rolling admissions. Check each school's rolling admissions start date. Some schools accept applications as early as the summer before the senior year. Under rolling admissions, colleges accept eligible candidates until all freshman spots are filled—so the earlier you apply, the better. Students typically receive the decision within two months after the completed application is sent in. Students who get accepted do not have to commit, and some schools give students until May 1 to make a decision.

Guaranteed Admissions
Offered by a number of public universities to students who meet certain academic and/or test score requirements. Students still need to apply, but qualified candidates typically get admissions offers earlier than other students.

Early Notification/Early Evaluation
An option offered to applicants by a limited number of selective institutions, designed to give students an idea of their chances for admission. This is not an admission plan, nor is it an offer of admission.

WHEN TO APPLY TO COLLEGES UTILIZING EARLY DECISION / EARLY ACTION

Only students who are absolutely certain they know which school they want to attend should apply Early Decision.

Early Action is a good option for students who would like to know whether they got into a school sooner rather than later. Students accepted under Early Action can typically wait until May 1 to decide where to enroll.

Benefits of applying early may include:
- Improving your chances of being accepted

- Improving your chances of getting a scholarship

- Getting first choice for housing

- Gaining time to prepare for college and study for high school classes/AP tests, if accepted

- Gaining more time to apply to other colleges with later deadlines if you get rejected

- Receiving peace of mind

Early Decision and Financial Aid

If you are admitted early, but you are unhappy with the financial aid awarded, you can make an appeal. Be careful of the drawback in doing this: Your high school is not permitted to send your transcripts to other colleges when an early decision offer is still in play. You may have to wait awhile for the college to process your appeal.

Chapter 3

Social Media, You, and College Admissions

I decided to add this chapter into the book sooner rather than later so you'd be able to get a head start on cleaning up your online presence.

College admissions officers use Facebook and Twitter! They read blogs, check out YouTube, and view Instagram photos and videos.

The horror stories are true of students being denied admission or scholarships thanks to something they posted online. Sports team coaches also like to check out potential athletes. Colleges and coaches want responsible students, not ones who may bring trouble. Don't be fooled into thinking "private" pages are private. The way online security keeps changing, your best bet is not to post anything you think can embarrass you.

Common sense is key.

Here are some general guidelines for keeping your admissions chances safe:

Do not write anything negative about colleges.
One student praised the school while visiting the campus then trashed it online. Admissions took notice, and the student was rejected.

Never post anything online that is incriminating or embarrassing. Ever.
Representatives have reported receiving anonymous Facebook and Google "tips" around admissions time, including photos of students doing things that they shouldn't be doing. On at least one occasion, a tip has caused an offer of admission to be revoked. (Some tips are called in by jealous classmates also vying for a top school.)

Check your "tags."
Check to see if any Facebook "friends" who have access to your profile have posted any unflattering comments or tagged any questionable photos with your name. If there is something you do not want to be connected to, you must untag yourself and talk to the person who posted the pictures and ask to have them taken down.

Remove your phone numbers and addresses from Facebook.
This makes it harder to do a search on you. It's a safety guideline as well.

Set privacy filters as strongly as possible.
But never assume that what you post will not be seen.

Use the "grandparent test."
If you wouldn't want your grandparents to see what was posted online, then it should not be posted. This goes for things on a personal wall or webpage, or someone else's. Make sure your friends know about this test policy, too. (If your grandparents happen to be wild and crazy folks, err on the side of conservative caution.)

Remove all photos and posts with anything questionable, including:

▸ Drinking and/or drugs, even if you're abstaining—this includes holding a cup of any kind

▸ Wild behavior, even if alcohol or drugs aren't in the picture

▸ Nudity

▸ Hints of sex or sexuality

▸ Interests that are questionable

▸ Favorite quotes that reference illegal activities

▸ Obscene or offensive language, gestures, or activities

▸ Bullying, cheating, or lying

▸ Controversial political ideas or expressions of support/disgust

31

▸ Anything else you might regret

Let your friends know not to post anything that might get you into trouble.

The Positive Side of Social Media
With the negatives come positives, too. There's an opportunity to present yourself positively. Online, you can distinguish yourself by showcasing your achievements and accomplishments, and/or revealing some of your goals and aspirations. Athletes can post highlight videos. Film students can post their work. Science students can present a project they are working on.

At International College Counselors, we encourage students to use their online presence and social networking tools to their advantage. Many colleges do look at student pages and blogs, especially if those students are being considered for a scholarship. The more prestigious the scholarship, the more they'll scrutinize.

Furthermore, students can use social media to express interest in the colleges to which they are applying. "Friend" a college's Facebook page, become a Twitter follower, or join a college's LinkedIn group. Students can even contact an admissions representative directly. If you do this, be polite and respectful of the rep's time. Some schools also offer social media outreach that lets prospective students interact with current students.

PROFESSIONALIZE YOUR EMAIL ADDRESS

If your email address begins with something silly or outrageous, it's time to open another email account, even if you only use it for college applications and jobs. Then, if you have to make up something, make up something nice like "johnincollege." A name like "gatorhater" should not be used to apply to the University of Florida, whose students are known as the Gators. Do not do this for any school. A memorable email address or your first and last name is better than a long string of numbers and letters. Make sure you check your inbox regularly so you don't miss anything from the colleges to which you've applied.

Chapter 4

Writing Essays

TIPS FOR WRITING THE COLLEGE ESSAY

The personal essay can help you improve your chances for admission.

Your essay may be as short as 150 words, but the words you choose can mean the difference between a "maybe" and a "yes." Your writing tells the admissions committee how and why you are different from everybody else.

While there is no exact formula for the perfect admission essay, here are some tips you should consider when trying to make a lasting impression on someone who reads fifty to a hundred essays a day:

Write about yourself.
The admissions committee isn't looking to learn about holidays or bioresearch, they're looking to learn about you—your achievements, your obstacles, your goals, your passions, your personality, your values, and your character. If you are asked to write about an influential person, the college wants to know his or her influence on you. Whatever topic you choose to center your essay around, make sure you shine through. You can use details about your country or customs, but only if they support the description of you.

Focus on one facet of yourself.
Admissions committees are looking for an in-depth essay. Pick one project, one activity, or one passion. Don't try to cover too many topics in your essay, or you'll end up with a laundry list of details and activities. The magic is in the details. Make the reader remember you.

Tell a good story.
You want to describe, not make a list. For example, demonstrate how

you are compassionate—don't just tell readers you are compassionate. If you had a difficulty, don't give the admissions committee a list of complaints or hardships; tell them how you overcame them.

Keep it real.
Don't make things up or try to come across as someone completely different from yourself. If you speak from the heart, it will show and your essay will flow more easily. Choosing something you've experienced will also give you the vivid and specific details the admissions committee is looking to see in your essay.

Share your opinions, but avoid anything controversial.
You don't know who is going to be reading your essay, so you want to appeal to the broadest audience possible. Write about something you like as opposed to something you don't. This is not the time or the place to share your opinions on what's wrong with a government or argue about religion. Don't speak badly of any people, concepts, or ideas.

Don't repeat information already in your application.
If you've taken six of the hardest courses in one year, don't list that you've done it or that you did it because you "love to learn," unless this relates directly to the focus of your essay. Admissions officers want to learn something about you from your essay that they can't learn from reading the other sections of your application.

Leverage your native culture, traditions, and experiences.
As an international applicant, don't try to "Americanize" or "mainstream" your application. Schools are looking for diversity. The goal is to stand out and not appear to be like all the other applicants.

Add a little something about the school.
Mention something specific about the school, especially something academic. For example, note whether you're interested in a certain major, program, track, or professor. Don't over-flatter the school or talk about generic features like a beautiful campus or dining hall. Adding something about the school's academic programs shows that you did

your research and there's a scholarly reason you're applying there.

Copy-and-paste carefully.

It's easier to tailor one essay for many schools than to write each one from scratch. Besides, most schools will ask similar questions: for example, why you want to attend or study a particular major. So you may do some cutting and pasting. However, read every essay over carefully, like it's the first one you wrote. Almost every admission officer can tell stories of students who accidentally wrote how excited they were by the opportunities offered at another school. Admissions officers understand that you are applying to more than just their college. However, this kind of mistake demonstrates carelessness, and they don't like that. Not one bit. Especially if you told the other college it was your first choice.

Avoid scientific words, acronyms, industry jargon, or foreign phrases.

Avoid using them if you can. Your essay needs to be easy for anyone to read. If the name of a club or a school magazine is not instantly recognizable for what it is, add a short description. You write for *The Eagle*. What is that? Describe *The Eagle* as the school literary magazine. As smart as admissions readers are, you also cannot assume that they know all the latest words or complex industry terms.

Avoid slang and shorthand.

Avoid using slang or technical language. The clearer you are with what you want to say, the better.

Avoid profanity.

Don't use any.

Spend time on your essay.

William Shakespeare didn't write his plays overnight, and neither should you write your essay overnight. The admission committee is looking to see what you can do given the time to brainstorm, rewrite, and polish. They are looking to see what topic you choose and what you do with it. An essay won't help you if it's sloppy and uninformative.

Check your grammar and spelling.
Yes, this counts. You can write conversationally, but the grammar and spelling still need to be correct. Don't solely rely on your computer's spell-checker or an online translation service. Oftentimes, the wrong word (spelled correctly) can slip by or the translation can be completely wrong. Nothing says last-minute essay more than the wrong spelling and grammar. If you are not fluent in English, ask someone who is fluent in English to review it.

Show the essay to someone who can give you objective feedback.
Sometimes you can get too close to the essay and be unable to see it clearly. Other people can often tell if there isn't enough being revealed, or your essay rambles, or if the humor is falling flat, or if you're not making the impression you'd want to. Remember, this essay will be read by someone who doesn't know you but who is going to be making a big decision based on what they'll learn from it.

COMMON APPLICATION ESSAYS

The Common Application is a single college application that students can complete and send to any number of participating colleges. For the 2017–18 application cycle, the Common Application asked students to choose one of the following essay prompts and write an essay of no more than 650 words:

- Some students have a background, identity, interest, or talent that is so meaningful they believe their application would be incomplete without it. If this sounds like you, then please share your story.

- The lessons we take from obstacles we encounter can be fundamental to later success. Recount a time when you faced a challenge, setback, or failure. How did it affect you, and what did you learn from the experience?

- Reflect on a time when you questioned or challenged a belief or idea. What prompted your thinking? What was the outcome?

- Describe a problem you've solved or a problem you'd like to solve. It can be an intellectual challenge, a research query, an ethical dilemma - anything that is of personal importance, no matter the scale. Explain its significance to you and what steps you took or could be taken to identify a solution.

- Discuss an accomplishment, event, or realization that sparked a period of personal growth and a new understanding of yourself or others.

- Describe a topic, idea, or concept you find so engaging that it makes you lose all track of time. Why does it captivate you? What or who do you turn to when you want to learn more?

- Share an essay on any topic of your choice. It can be one you've already written, one that responds to a different prompt, or one of your own design.

In all of these essay prompts, students should find the key words and focus on these. Some key words that should start your thoughts include "background, identity, interest, or talent," "story," "failure...to success," "what did you learn," "challenged," "problem...solved," "significance to you," "solution," "accomplishment," "period of personal growth," "learn more," etc.

How to Start an Essay

Start with an idea of what you want to say. Remember your audience—a college that values academics, civic engagement, and cultural sensitivity. Maybe you want to talk about your volunteer work or growing up as a member of a minority group. Write, write, and keep writing. Don't worry about word count. Don't worry if you stray from your original thought. Don't worry about oversharing or going into too much detail. When your brain runs dry, read over what you wrote. Pick out the things you think sound interesting. Then see how you can work with what you've written to meet the essay's guidelines.

THE OPTIONAL ESSAY

Optional essays are not optional. Some students believe that they can skip the optional essay, that it's one of those "trick questions." Don't opt out.

If you are unsure about what to include, talk to your parents, a college counselor, a teacher, or a mentor.

Typically, I recommend that students explain their personal circumstances in the optional essay/additional information and use the main essay to highlight other, more positive experiences—unless the challenge was life-changing. I also recommend leaving some details out. For example, if you faced a challenge that did not reflect significantly on your schoolwork or extracurricular activities, you may want to leave this out. One essay that comes to mind was one I read about an eating disorder. The struggle was a major part of her life, but it would have distracted an admissions officer from her other accomplishments.

INTERNATIONAL COLLEGE COUNSELORS TIP:
Always think about what information you want colleges to know and use when evaluating your application. This should guide you in what to share. Don't share anything that does not make you look good, unless you absolutely have to, or unless you can turn it around to show the positive.

Writing about setbacks: What do you say? How do you say it?
If your grades or involvement in activities dropped significantly at some point in your high school career, somewhere in your application you need to explain why. You can explain this in the main essay or in the section called "additional information." Many colleges leave space for the descriptions of unusual circumstances.

Whatever you do, do not turn your essay into something designed to make someone feel sorry for you. Many other students have had to deal with real hardships, too.

The essay you write should demonstrate to colleges that despite the challenges you faced, you were able to stay focused and to overcome them. Admissions officers want an explanation of the situation, but just as important is how you dealt with it.

If you talk about a challenge, it has to truly have affected you while in high school. Moving to another country or having to work two jobs to support your family while attending school is something to share. Getting sick and missing a few tests is not. Trying to make something major out of something minor can demonstrate weak judgment. If you provide no explanation for a sudden grade drop, the admissions officers will make their own conclusions. However, this will not work in your favor.

Own up to any bad behavior.
Don't lie about school punishments. Your high school is duty-bound to report them. And don't pretend your suspension for underage drinking was a one-time thing if you had two warnings beforehand. This will also be reported. What matters to the college is how you processed your experience. Colleges want to see that you accept responsibility for your actions, show sincere remorse, and/or can talk about what lessons you've learned. From our experience, a student who admits wrongdoing in an honest and apologetic way can be extremely successful with college admissions.

ANSWERING THE QUIRKY QUESTIONS

In recent years, a number of colleges have been adding quirky questions to their applications. These supplemental questions are considered a way to get students to stand out from the crowd.

These questions have included:

- "It's not easy being green" was a frequent lament of Kermit the Frog. Discuss.

- Imagine you have to wear a costume for a year of your life. What would you pick and why?

- What is your favorite ride at the amusement park? How does this reflect your approach to life?

- What does Play-Doh have to do with Plato?

- What would you do with a free afternoon tomorrow?

- What was your favorite thing about last Tuesday?

- "I learned to make my mind large, as the universe is large, so that there is room for paradoxes." —Maxine Hong Kingston. What paradoxes do you live with?

- According to Henry David Thoreau, "One is not born into the world to do everything, but to do something." What is your something?

What colleges are looking for is your voice. Use this as an opportunity to demonstrate your "out of the box" thinking. However, don't go overboard. Admissions officers are looking to see whether you'll be an interesting person to have on campus. Interesting means imaginative, not crazy and not dangerous-sounding.

GREAT FIRST SENTENCES

You need a great hook and a great first sentence. Opening sentences have the power to compel and fascinate. Some of our favorite student essay first sentences include:

- *For eight years, I have celebrated polyester.*

- *I vividly recall coming home from school one day in Buenos Aires, Argentina, to find my house in disarray and my parents packing one suitcase after another.*

- *I'll admit it: I have a thing for gavels—a thing for motions and seconds and the clarity that they bring to meetings.*

- *I eagerly reached into my Hello Kitty backpack.*

- *Max prances in place as we await our turn into the arena.*

- *Drip. Drip. Drip. Tick. Tick. Tick. As I lie in the hospital, waiting to be taken into surgery, I can only think that my IV drip sounds just like a metronome.*

You want to read more, right?

FATAL ESSAY ERRORS

Application essays have been requested as part of the college application for many, many years. The admissions teams have seen a lot of "creativity." Here are their least favorite types of essays:

- Metaphor. Don't compare yourself to a mango, a Ferris wheel, or any other object.

- Death. Don't write about a person or pet's death unless it truly affected your life and you can use it to show your growth—for example, if someone died of cancer and you made it your mission to raise money/awareness, or if a death during high school affected your grades and caused you to stumble, but then you regrouped to overcome.

- Free-verse essays, essays written as raps, limericks, etc. Don't emphasize form over function.

- "Meta" essays, in which you talk about writing an essay, about the process of writing an essay, or about essays themselves.

Additionally, you should avoid writing about the topics below unless you have something extraordinary to say:

- A trip abroad

- Generic admiration for your mom or dad

- The controversial rock star or movie star whom you idolize

42

- Overcoming an injury and making an athletic comeback
- Understanding the meaning of life from a fishing trip

Sorry, but thousands of students have beat you to these topics and they are oftentimes found to be quite boring. These are called "cliché essays" because the reader knows from the start just where you are going with it.

THE VIDEO COLLEGE ESSAY

A number of college admissions departments are accepting video college essays.

The first step for any student is to view recent videos and see what others have done. This will give you an idea of the range of possibilities.

When it comes to actually making your own video, it's important to be original but in a way that is comfortable for you. Do what works for you. Your main goal needs to be communicating your message.

- Start by identifying the question and any directions.
- Think about what you want to say.
- Write a script that is clear on the message and ideas you want to get across.
- Collect resources and props that you want to use in the video.
- Record the video until it's as perfect as possible. Some students record the video themselves using a tripod and speaking directly into the camera; others enlist the services of a friend or family member.
- Review your video and collect feedback.
- Edit, edit, edit, and re-record if necessary.
- Get more feedback.

▸   Edit and re-record until it's as perfect as it can be. Make sure it fits the requested length and meets all specifications before sending it in.

If your English language skills are not strong, we do not recommend that you use a video essay or statement for admissions.

TRUTH, PLAGIARISM, AND THE CONSEQUENCES ON COLLEGE APPLICATIONS AND ESSAYS

No matter how desperately you want to get into a school, don't lie on the college application. If a university finds out you lied on an application or essay—even a little—you will get rejected, almost guaranteed.

How does a school know when a student does not tell the truth on their college application? Colleges are doing research of their own. A common practice is for college admissions officers to call up high schools to verify a student's activities and awards. College admissions officers have also called employers, internship organizers, and places where students have performed public service. They are also looking applicants up online.

Thanks to the Internet, it's easy to see if a student really has received a major award or a significant ranking, whether it's in music or sports. Some universities like MIT even hire private investigators to check up on student claims. While there is always a chance you won't be caught, do you really want to risk it?

Embellishing the truth isn't particularly good, either. If you delivered meals to homebound senior citizens in their community, don't write that you ended world hunger. Certainly, there's nothing wrong with presenting yourself in a positive way. This is where students can balance using clever adjectives, but you also must remember to be ethical.

Plagiarism is always wrong, and schools are getting better at detecting it. Stanford and Penn State, for example, are using an admissions essay service offered by Turnitin. This software service is used by a number of professors to check their students' classwork, and it has proven to be a big success. College application essays are now being compared to a huge database of collected information and what's already on the web. While most schools don't publicize whether or not they use this detection system, students have been rejected because of plagiarism on the college application.

College essays are about the student: who they are, not who they're not. I truly believe that every student has a gem of an essay within them. What they need to do is find that ounce of truth and turn it into a ton of good, positive writing. Remember to proofread.

Chapter 5

Letters of Recommendation

One of the most important parts of your college application isn't even written by you, and that's the letters of recommendation.

Do not wait until the last minute to request these. You should actually be working on getting letters of recommendation from the minute you start your final school year.

You want the college admissions officers to know that a teacher or other recommender is really recommending you for a school, not just doing it without any feeling or thought.

WHOM SHOULD YOU ASK FOR A LETTER OF RECOMMENDATION?

When it comes to choosing whom to ask, you want adults—unrelated to you—who know you well enough to write something special about you. Most private colleges want one counselor and two teacher recommendations. And many of these colleges request that at least one of the recommenders be a teacher from a core subject (math, English, social studies, science, or foreign language).

The best recommendations provide insight about you and knowledge of your high school success, so you want to ask people who can write about your talents, abilities, and more. For example, teachers can comment about your academic skills, but it's better if they can comment on your personality, too.

Believe it or not, admissions officers have seen the same letter for different students—with the names changed, needless to say. What happened is that more than one student from a school applied to the same college and asked the same teacher for a recommendation. Apparently, the teacher didn't know either student too well and wrote something generic and uninspired.

So choose a teacher who knows you over a teacher who gave you top grades, or one whom you think can "write well." For example, your English teacher may write the best, but a strong letter of recommendation supporting you goes a lot further than a letter that has perfect grammar, but no substance.

Choose the person you ask wisely and carefully. Make sure you choose someone who likes you. If you ask a teacher, make sure it's in a class where you have great attendance and few or no tardies, actively participate in class, are well behaved, and get good grades. You may not even see the letter that is written about you, so it needs to be from someone you feel comfortable with. Additionally, at least one of the recommendation letters should come from a teacher who taught you during your junior or senior year in a core subject.

On the Common Application, you are not able to make changes to the teacher/counselor list after you submit your application, with the exception of resending the notification to your teacher or counselor. So make sure before you push the submit button that you have wisely selected your recommenders.

INTERNATIONAL COLLEGE COUNSELORS TIP:
Almost all schools ask for a counselor recommendation. Be sure to get to know your counselor and provide her with the information she needs to know about you.

TRANSLATING LETTERS OF RECOMMENDATION

Most colleges require letters of recommendation to be in English. If the person giving you a recommendation does not speak English as a first language and has trouble writing in English, have them write the recommendation in their native language. You will then need to send the letter of recommendation to a professional translator and have it translated into English. When submitting the recommendation, send the translated recommendation with the original recommendation.

It is better to have a strongly translated recommendation in the original language than a poorly written one in English. Sometimes, a college will accept a letter of recommendation in the original language (like Spanish), but each college has different policies, so check with each of your targeted schools about their requirements.

TREND ALERT: PARENT RECOMMENDATIONS

A small number of colleges are welcoming letters of recommendation from parents. The colleges that do this are looking for parents to bring a new dimension to candidates whose full personality may otherwise be captured only with grades, test scores, and traditional recommendation letters from teachers and guidance counselors. Only a few colleges want these; if a college does not ask for this, do not send in a parent-written recommendation.

HOW TO ASK FOR A LETTER OF RECOMMENDATION

Carefully read the instructions on what kind of letters of recommendation each school requires. Some applications require two letters of recommendation from teachers and one recommendation from your guidance or college counselor. Other applications ask for one teacher recommendation and one counselor recommendation, or that you choose teachers from specific subjects like math. Other applications allow you to choose an employer or a friend. Make sure you follow the directions!

Start early.
Two months before an application deadline, start asking for your letters of recommendation. Your recommender needs time to write a thoughtful and articulate letter. Consider asking teachers prior to the summer before your senior year. This will give them plenty of time to write something reflective and complete.

Make an appointment to speak with your recommenders.
Don't just thrust the letter template into a teacher's hand in the five minutes you have between classes. Making an appointment shows that you're respectful of their time.

Help your recommender.
At your meeting, make sure you give those chosen people everything they might need to write your letter and submit it on time. By giving recommenders what they need, your letter will, more likely, be properly detailed. This also demonstrates to your recommender that you are taking this process seriously and that you appreciate their time and effort.

Be careful about sending a teacher your résumé. You want him or her to write about you as a student in a particular class. You don't want them listing your activities.

Follow up.
Remember, your recommenders are doing you a favor. Show your appreciation by sending a thank-you note.

Chapter 6

Interviewing and Résumés

There are two types of college interviews.

One is a formal or traditional interview. This interview takes place on or off campus with a dean or an admissions officer. Generally, the interviewer will ask you questions and you will answer them. The school wants to get a sense of you, find out how much thinking you have done about college, and learn how well you express yourself and perform in an interview situation.

The second is the informal or alumni interview. This interview is more conversational. In an informal interview, the interviewer wants to get a sense of your interests and how well you would fit in on campus.

It's important to know which type of interview(s) a school has.

Practice and knowing what to expect will help you through both kinds of interviews.

Many colleges no longer require interviews, but interviews can give a student the edge if the school is forced to choose between closely matched applicants.

ARE INTERVIEWS REQUIRED?

Each school has different requirements. Not every college you apply to will require an interview. However, do not assume a school does not require an interview.

Read your application materials closely to see if an interview is required or recommended.

No two schools are exactly alike. At many schools, interviews don't count toward admissions. Their interviews are "informative."

Other schools have an evaluative interview, which means they "count." If an interview is not required but recommended, pursue it.

However, we don't always recommend the interview for our students. If you are exceptionally shy, insecure, cannot speak English well, or really truly believe your nervousness or lack of social skills will make a poor impression, do not go on an interview unless it is mandatory. It is better to let your application do the talking for you. While an interview can help, it can also hurt an applicant.

SETTING UP AN INTERVIEW

Some colleges want the students to call them or fill out an online form to set up the interview. So the first thing you need to do is call the admissions office or check online to find out what the school interview policy is.

The interview should take place before the application deadline, November or December for most schools. The interview appointment should be set about one month before you plan to do the interview. Two, three, or even four months in advance works, too. It's better to err on the early side. The worst that can happen is that the school will tell you it's too early to make an appointment and they'll tell you when to call back. Some schools, like Yale, have a limited number of on-campus interviews that are available on a first-come, first-serve basis. Again, make sure you check the admissions requirements and interview procedures of each individual school.

The On-Campus Interview
Plan the interview to coincide with a college visit. Even if you decide not to apply to the school, it's good practice. If the school is far away, this arrangement can also save money on travel costs.

If at all possible, schedule the interview for after your school tour. The next day is ideal, but if you're on a tight schedule, you can even arrange it for a few hours after you take the tour. This way you'll have intelligent questions and answers for your interview. Weekdays are better than weekends for both an interview and a campus tour, because lots more will be going on.

INTERNATIONAL COLLEGE COUNSELORS TIP:
Go on your first interviews at your least-favorite colleges. It's the best way to get practice.

The Alumni Interview
Different schools have different ways of arranging alumni interviews. Your chances of being asked to attend one really depends on how organized your area's alumni are and whether the school counts the interview.

The sooner you submit the application, the greater the chances of being offered an alumni interview. To increase the likelihood of being contacted for an interview, you should submit your application at least one month ahead of the deadline.

Each year, the first interview assignments are typically sent out to local alumni chapters in early September. Early Decision applicants should expect to hear something about their interview by mid-November. Otherwise, the general rule is that Regular Decision applicants may be contacted as late as mid-February/early March.

Whether you are contacted or not may also depend on where you live. International students or students who live in remote areas may need to do an interview over the phone, via Skype, or skip it altogether. The best way to be sure is to contact the school yourself and ask the admissions office how the alumni interview process works—and if it counts toward admission.

If the school gives you the name of the regional person who sets up the interviews, call or email that person. Then give your alumnus time to respond (five business days). These are volunteers who are often busy with career and family. If you still haven't received a response after five business days, contact the admissions office for a different alumnus on the list.

If your school of choice only offers informational interviews, you may need to be the one to initiate the process. Whether or not you are offered an interview may be more dependent on the enthusiasm and schedules of local alumni than whether the school is seriously considering you.

If the policy of the college is to contact the student and you don't get offered an informational interview, this may not be a reflection on you or your application. Many colleges, including some Ivies, have no prescreening process for interviews. They try to reach every applicant.

If you have not heard from a much-wanted school, you need to find out whether you can request an interview. Some schools do not allow interview requests, while others, like Duke, do. Again, call the school admissions office or go online to see what the college policy is. If the school does allow you to request an interview, they will tell you what the next steps are.

If you've already been contacted by an alum for a mandatory evaluative interview (one that counts), make sure you prepare, show up on time, and send a thank-you note.

Admissions offices know that not every applicant will be contacted for an interview, and they will not hold this against a candidacy.

INTERNATIONAL COLLEGE COUNSELORS TIP:
Students need to know the alumni interview policy of the colleges about which they are serious. Many universities have limited alumni who will interview, and so interviews are on a first-come, first-serve basis. The earlier you send in your application, the better chances you

have of getting an interview.

The Video Interview

Some schools accept video interviews that are done through a company like InitialView. The company will interview you live and then upload a video. The video will then be shared with multiple colleges of your choice. The interviews are viewed by the schools both to "meet" you and to determine your English-speaking ability.

You may arrange an interview with InitialView. The information is on their website at http://new.initialview.com/.

Note that an InitialView interview is not college-specific and therefore the interviewer is unlikely to be able to answer a specific college's questions. There is a cost for this service.

Before making an interview video, call the college you are applying to or check its website to see whether they accept video interviews.

INTERNATIONAL COLLEGE COUNSELORS TIP:

If the interviewing fee is prohibitive, fee waivers are available at many colleges.

PREPARING FOR THE COLLEGE INTERVIEW: BEFORE THE INTERVIEW

Interviewers are looking for well-presented and well-researched honesty. Here's how to achieve that.

Outline the answers to questions the interviewer will most likely ask.

Some common interview questions include:

- ▸ Why do you want to attend this university?
- ▸ What do you know about our university?

- What do you want to get out of your college experience?

- What could you contribute to our college community?

- Is this school your first choice and why?

- What other schools are you applying to?

- What major(s) are you interested in?

- What classes do you like the best at your high school and why?

- What extracurricular activities are you most involved in?

- What have you liked or disliked about your school? What would you change?

- What was your favorite job/internship/volunteer experience and why?

- What do you expect to be doing ten years from now?

- How have you been a leader or demonstrated leadership?

- What about you is unique?

- How would your friends describe you?

- What are your greatest strengths and weaknesses?

- Describe a difficult choice you had to make and how you handled it.

- What has been your proudest life achievement so far?

- What book/film/television show has made the biggest impact on you?

- Who is the most influential person in your life?

- Is there anything else you want to add?

Some uncommon, but sometimes asked, college interview questions include:

▸ If you could be any animal, what would you be and why?

▸ What are three words that describe you?

▸ When do you feel the most proud of yourself?

▸ If you could be any type of fruit, what would you be and why?

▸ What is your favorite color?

▸ If you could trade places with any other person for a week, famous or not famous, living or dead, real or fictional, with whom would it be?

▸ If Hollywood made a movie about your life, what actor or actress would play you?

▸ If you were a car, what kind of car would you be?

▸ What can our college offer you that another college cannot?

▸ If you had a thousand dollars to give away, what would you do with it?

Do research!
Good answers require research. Do research on the college. Know why you want to attend. Know which programs and extracurricular activities in which you are interested in participating and why. If there are faculty members of interest or graduates who inspire you, mention them.

Also prepare by thinking of times when you have been successful. Make a list of your skills and interests as well as your strengths and weaknesses. Be familiar with your own résumé.

Practice. Practice. Practice.
Practice will make you better (but you don't need to be perfect). Prepare answers to commonly asked interview questions. But don't try to memorize them or you will probably come off as stilted, unnatural,

and over-rehearsed.

Practice with a parent or a friend and videotape your session. Afterward, replay the interview and see how well you did. Some specific things to consider include:

- Your responses. Are they clear and understandable or vague and uncertain?

- Your give-and-take. Are your answers too short or too long?

- Your engagement. Do you have a good handshake, good eye contact, a nice smile?

- Your speech. Are you talking too fast, too slowly, too quietly, or too loudly? Do you say "um," "you know," or "like" too frequently?

- Your posture. Are you transmitting interest?

Pull together a list of thoughtful questions to ask the interviewer. Good questions include: "What is the personality of this college as you've experienced it? What kind of student is happy here? What kind of student is not happy here? What are some of the best features of the school? Why did you choose to work here?"

Offer to send a résumé to the interviewer before the interview. By doing this, he or she can be more familiar with your accomplishments, and conversation will be easier for both of you.

WHAT TO WEAR TO A COLLEGE INTERVIEW

In addition to your good, well-thought-out answers, you need to winningly present yourself in dress and social skills. Spend time preparing your appearance and your presentation. An interviewee should look, not only sound, impressive. The big picture of any student for a school is that you will be a representative of them.

Wear the right clothes, as in "dress for success."
The key is to dress in a manner that suggests you are serious and taking the meeting seriously. It's about putting your best foot forward and showing respect, enthusiasm, and interest in a formal atmosphere. This being said, avoid jeans, shorts, tank tops, flip-flops, sandals, Crocs, or anything that's too tight, too short, too provocative, or too revealing.

Given that, you also need to feel comfortable and confident. For men, a safe list of clothes includes khakis, a light blue or white collared shirt, and a jacket. For women, a nice blouse, a long skirt or pants, and possibly a jacket. Showing a flash of your own style is nice as long as it doesn't include anything provocative or profane. And, please, clothes do need to be neat, not as if you fell out of bed and into yesterday's clothes.

Sure, you can always argue that if a college doesn't like the way you are, maybe the college isn't for you. Remind yourself that focusing too much on "being yourself" in an interview can take away from what is far more important to universities, and that is who you will become.

And if you do decide to wear a tank top and very short shorts and the interview goes sour and the college rejects you, then, yes, the college wasn't for you.

Of course, if you have a brilliant transcript, sterling SAT scores, and international recognition, those will surpass even the scruffiest of looks.

Then again, here are some real deal-breakers that some college admissions officers swear they've seen. Students who:

▸   Arrive barefoot.

▸   Obviously haven't showered in days.

▸   Sit on the floor, rather than in the chair provided.

▸   Put their feet up on the couch, chair, desk, or coffee table.

- Pick their noses (or any other part of their body) during the interview.

- Swear during the interview.

- Answer a cell phone or send text messages.

- Wear earphones, sunglasses, or hats the entire time.

- Bring along the family pet.

DURING THE INTERVIEW

During the interview, you want to be professional, engaging, positive, and enthusiastic at all times. Furthermore, and just as importantly:

- Smile.

- Look the interviewer in the eye.

- Show up to the interview on time. "On time" means ten to fifteen minutes early.

- Do not chew gum, eat, or slouch.

- Do not wear too much perfume or cologne.

- Turn off your cell phone. Not set on vibrate. Off.

- Do not use generational slang or language that would be inappropriate in a business setting.

- Avoid giving "yes," "no," or one-word answers. In answering any question, you want to offer details. If you're asked what your favorite high school subject was, reply with more information than the one-word "science." Did you prefer biology, chemistry, or physics? Explain why you liked it best. Start a conversation that almost every interviewer can enjoy.

- If the interviewer asks you what other colleges you are considering, don't be afraid to offer up a name or two. Do offer good, logical reasoning on why you like the interviewer's college better.

▸ At the end of the interview, leave the interviewer with two or three points you want him or her to remember you by. A good ending: "I am very passionate about astronomy, have done my homework on colleges, and know that this school is the best school for me."

▸ Before leaving, shake the interviewer's hand and thank him or her for the opportunity to meet.

▸ Endnote: Be who you are—but a little bit better, better dressed, and more well-mannered.

WHAT TO REMEMBER FOR A COLLEGE INTERVIEW

Résumés

Bring two copies of your résumé so you'll be ready if the interviewer asks you to share your experiences and accomplishments. The second copy is for the interviewer. See the end of this chapter for how to write a high school résumé. Place the résumé in a padfolio or a large, clean manila envelope.

The Interviewer's Name

One of the top interviewing mistakes is not remembering the name of the interviewer. Make sure you remember with whom you are meeting.

The Interviewer's Phone Number

If for some reason you run into an emergency or you are running late, you can attempt to contact the interviewer to tell them of your situation.

The Interview Location's Name and Directions

You do not want to get lost.

Women may carry a nice, simple purse while men may bring a nice, clean messenger-style bag.

WHAT *NOT* TO BRING TO A COLLEGE INTERVIEW

Your parents. Parents should never, ever sit in on the interview. Neither should siblings, cousins, friends, or dogs—unless it is a service dog, and even then you should ask ahead. There is a chance the interviewer may be allergic.

AFTER THE INTERVIEW

Follow up!
The impression you make does not end when the interview ends. If you interviewed with someone from your home country, write a handwritten thank-you note after your interview to show you are a professional, polite person who values the interviewer's time. A thank-you note also offers the opportunity to reiterate key points you made during your interview.

If you are worried about your country's postal system or you interviewed with someone in another country, these days email works as well. You want the interviewer to know that you appreciate his or her time.

In your note, reference something in the interview that you talked about so it doesn't look like a generic thank-you note you send to everyone.

Here is a sample email/note:

Formal Interview Follow-Up

***

Dear Mr./Ms. [LAST NAME OF INTERVIEWER],

Thank you for taking the time out of your busy schedule to meet with me. I enjoyed meeting with you and learning more about [NAME OF COLLEGE].

Per our conversation, I am extremely interested in attending [NAME OF COLLEGE]. I enjoyed hearing about why you chose to attend [NAME OF COLLEGE] and how it has helped make you the person that you are today. Your candor and passion have further solidified my desire to attend. I especially enjoyed learning about [Insert an interesting fact here that the interviewer told you].

I strongly believe that I will be a great fit at [NAME OF COLLEGE]. Thank you again for taking the time to meet with me and answering all my questions.

Sincerely,

[Your name]

***

POST-THANK YOU NOTE

If you tell the admissions counselor or alum you'll get in touch with him or her again, then you need to do it. We recommend that you keep any follow-ups short and positive. Let the admissions office know of any new achievements. Don't send emails asking them for answers to questions you can find somewhere else, like on the college website.

HOW TO WRITE A HIGH SCHOOL RÉSUMÉ

Writing a high school résumé for college admissions is different from writing one for work. The best advice is to keep it simple. You want to create a concise and easy-to-read document that best presents your accomplishments. The college admissions teams will not be impressed with fancy type unless you're applying to art school.

Create a list.
Start with the ninth grade and make note of all activities, honors, memberships, and enrichment programs by quarter. Don't leave off summers.

Organize into major categories.
Next organize the information into major categories: honors, extra-curricular activities, community service, sports, enrichment, special skills, and work experience. Sometimes the information "categories" are listed on college applications.

Organize into subcategories.
Organize the individual entries by category and date. Be specific about positions, titles, organizations, and locations. Do not use acronyms; for example, write out "Miami Beach Senior High School" instead of "MBSH."

Include special skills and certifications.
Make sure you include any special skills and certifications. They show accomplishment and offer an indication of deeper interest in an activity. For example, if you are in a swimming-instruction program, list your Red Cross Lifeguard certification. If you can speak more than one language, list them. If you practice tae kwon do, add the belt level you've reached.

On the Common Application, you should add these skills to the Activities section.

Format the information.

Format the information on a document in a way you think is clear and attractive. On the top of the page, put your name, address, cell and home phone numbers, and email address. Ideally the résumé will be one page long. Make sure it is no longer than two pages.

Sample Résumé

Ryan Mylez
Apartado Aéreo 17, Bogotá, Colombia
Phone: +571 5551539; Email: ryanmylez@xyz.co

Education
Colegio Fontán
Address
Phone Number
Expected Graduation Date: [Month/Year]
Cumulative GPA:
SAT/ACT Score:

Honors, Awards, and Distinctions
Math Honor Society—VP 12, Member 11
Colegio Fontán Basketball Team—MVP & Captain 12
Colegio Fontán Honor Roll—9, 10, 11
Winner of the International College Counselors Essay
Scholarship—11
Short story featured in *Teen Ink*—11
AP Scholar Award—11
Chatham University's Rachel Carson Book Award—11

Sample Résumé (continued)

Extracurricular Activities
International Club—Founder and President 11, 12
20 weeks per year, 2 hours per week
—Was selected to represent Colegio Fontán at the International Conference in Cali, 12.

Varsity Basketball Team—9, 10, 11, 12
35 weeks per year, 10 hours per week
—Played starting power forward for Colegio Fontán's basketball team. Averaged 8.4 points per game and 1.6 assists per game.

Math tutor—11, 12
20 weeks per year, 2 hours per week
—Tutored students in Algebra and Algebra II.

Writer for *El Heraldo*, the school newspaper—11, 12
35 weeks per year, 2 hours per week
—Wrote monthly stories and articles about current events.

Chess Club—9, 10, 11
20 weeks per year, 1 hour per week
—Attended monthly meetings, competed in in-school chess matches.

Community Service Club—9, 10, 11, 12
25 weeks per year, 1 hour per week
—Organized food drives and participated in fund-raising and charity events.

Sample Résumé (continued)

Employment
Hospital Universitario San Ignacio—11, 12
25 weeks per year, 4–8 hours per week
—Interned in the Magnetic Resonance Imaging Department, learned how to use MRIs and evaluate images, explored the working experience of doctors.

Alta Vista Sports Store—10
25 weeks per year, 10 hours per week
—Worked as a salesperson, customer service representative, and cashier.

Summer Activities
Summer Journalism Institute at the University of Florida—12
—Selected to attend a one-week intensive workshop in storytelling, editing, designing, photography, and multimedia.

Study-Abroad in the UK through Choate Rosemary Hall—11
—Participated in a five-week immersion program. Attended three courses taught in English.

YMCA Basketball Camp Counselor—10 (8 weeks), 11 (4 weeks)
—Led a group of 7–12-year-old children. Taught basketball skills, coordinated games, and counseled them during the summer.

Chapter 7

Standardized Tests

L ike it or not, the SAT/ACT will most likely help to determine which colleges you will be able to attend. Don't discount the test as simply one of many factors that will be considered, or believe that it is not very important. The reality is that unless you are a professional-level athlete or a math whiz with a Nobel Prize, the SAT/ACT will likely play a major role in your college admissions.

It makes sense to get the highest score possible.

In this chapter, we will also discuss the PSAT, SAT Subject Tests, the TOEFL (Test of English as a Foreign Language), the IELTS (International English Language Test System), and the CLEP (College-Level Examination Program).

THE PSAT

You don't have to take this test. But you should if you can.

The PSAT is the best practice for the SAT. It's a standardized test created by the College Board, the same company that creates the SAT, and it tests the same three subjects as the SAT: Evidence-Based Reading, Math, and Writing & Language. The kinds of questions and the directions are almost exactly the same as the SAT. You get to experience sitting down for a two- to three-hour test with few breaks. For many, it's an eye-opener.

PSAT scores indicate how you might do on each section on the SAT. Using the test results, you can then focus your test review on the areas and types of questions on which you most need to improve. Scores can also be used as a gauge to see what kind of additional study aids or tutoring is needed. Consider poor results as an early warning signal that serious work may be needed before you take the real SAT.

By taking the PSAT, you can also see how your performance on the SAT might compare with that of other students. This may boost self-esteem or be a good dose of reality/motivation.

Students outside the United States must make arrangements with a local school to register for and take the PSAT. The College Board recommends that international students register up to four months in advance of the test. For a list of schools offering the test go to https://ordering.collegeboard.org/testordering/publicSearch.

THE ACT AND SAT

How early is too early to study for the SAT and ACT? Freshmen and sophomores: It's not too early.

When should you start studying for the SAT and ACT?
a. Now
b. Immediately
c. Forthwith
d. All of the above

Answer: d. For "definitely."

It's never too early to start studying for the SAT or ACT. Do not plan on cramming for these critical tests. These tests are scored on a curve, and students are taking the tests worldwide.

Students who finish their exams in their junior year are always the happiest and usually the most successful.

Juniors: Take your standardized tests. Procrastination time is *over*. Juniors: *Finish* all standardized tests *this year*. This includes the ACT/SAT/TOEFL/IELTS and Subject Tests.

Waiting until the fall is almost always a bad idea.

▸ It makes choosing an Early Decision school extremely difficult.

▸ Students cannot apply in August to rolling admissions schools.

▸ If an emergency arises on the day of the test, or you're sick, or your car breaks down, there will be no time to take the test again. If your emergency happens on the last possible test date, you're truly out of luck—your bad score may be the one you'll have to live with.

Sure, college counselors will agree there's no point in taking a standardized test if you aren't ready, but most of you reading this now will have enough time to prepare.

For more details on the SAT and ACT tests, go online or take a look at all the resources out there. For SAT test prep, we highly recommend *The Official SAT Study Guide* by the College Board. For ACT test prep, we recommend *The Real ACT Prep Guide*. These are the only books we know of that feature official practice tests created by the test makers. The most recent edition will have the most up-to-date information.

How many times should I take the SAT and ACT?
This is the inevitable question. There is no magic number. But I will say that students should take the test AT LEAST two times, ideally more. Students fear that admissions officers will look at taking the test three or four times as too many and then penalize the student. This is not the case. I have never heard of a school rejecting a student for taking the test four times.

Even if they ask to see all scores, most schools will only consider the top scores. They pull the top ACT score and top SAT score in each of the categories, and that's it. So, if you're trying to get within a school's range, and you're off by a few hundred points in the SAT, it's definitely worth it to keep trying.

Of the schools that look at all the scores, usually admissions officers consider taking the test multiple times to be a sign of initiative, especially if you keep increasing your score. However, if you keep taking the test and you're doing poorer or plateauing, this is not a good thing. You need to regroup and consider tutoring or other study aids.

Each time you take the test, you should have studied and feel prepared that you're going to do well and increase your score from the previous time.

DIFFERENCES BETWEEN ACT AND SAT AND WHICH TO TAKE

Most colleges don't prefer one test over the other. The key is to figure out which one is best suited to your standardized testing strengths. Each test emphasizes different test-taking skills and tests your familiarity in different subjects.

Here are some facts about the ACT and SAT:

The ACT

▸ Is designed to evaluate your overall educational development and your ability to complete college-level work.

▸ Has four multiple-choice subject tests covering English, Math, Reading, and Science. Each content area is approached in one big chunk, with the optional Writing Test at the end.

▸ Includes an optional 30-minute writing test designed to measure your skill in planning and writing a short essay. If you opt to take it, the additional scores will be listed separately.

▸ Has 215 questions.

▸ You'll have 2 hours and 55 minutes, not including breaks or the 30-minute optional essay.

▸ There is no penalty for incorrect answers; only correct responses count. So there is no penalty for guessing.

- Subject test scores (ranging from 1 to 36) are determined by correct answers. The four areas are then averaged together to come up with your overall, or composite, score.

- Students may use a calculator on the ACT Math section. ACT Math covers Arithmetic, Algebra, Geometry, Algebra II, and Trigonometry. The science section tests logical reasoning based on data and scientific terms and is not based on classroom science.

- ACT questions are said to be more straightforward and easier to understand on a first read than those on the SAT.

The SAT

- Is designed to be more predictive of success in college and beyond.

- Content areas (Evidence-Based Reading and Writing, Math, and Optional Essay) are broken up into four required sections (2 math sections, 1 reading section, and 1 writing section).

- Includes an optional 50-minute essay.

- Has 154 questions.

- You will have 3 hours to complete the test, or 3 hours and 30 minutes with the optional essay.

- Test scores range from 400 to 1600, combining test results from two 800-point sections.

- The SAT Math has two sections, one calculator section and one no-calculator section.

- Evidence-Based Reading only features long passage questions based on U.S. and world literature, science, history, and social science and founding documents or written works of great global conversation.

- SAT Writing is similar to the Evidence-Based Reading section. This section prompts students to analyze evidence, cite information, and analyze data.

- There is no penalty for incorrect answers; only correct responses count. So there is no penalty for guessing.

- The optional essay uses a scale of 2–8 points. The essay prompts students to analyze evidence and explain how the author builds a persuasive argument.

- SAT questions are said to be more evidence- and context-based in an effort to focus on real-world situations and multi-step problem-solving.

Almost all competitive colleges "cherry-pick" (or "superscore") SAT sub-scores, meaning they consider the best combination of Math, Evidence-Based Reading and Writing, and Essay scores earned on different dates. Although increasing, fewer colleges do this with the four ACT sub-scores.

INTERNATIONAL COLLEGE COUNSELORS TIP:
Take practice tests to see which test you prefer. As all colleges accept scores from both the SAT and ACT, consider taking both tests to see which one you perform better on.

STUDY AIDS

There are many types of test preparation materials available. Some are free. Check out all of the options that exist.

Books
There are many books written to help you tackle the SAT and ACT. Head to your local bookstore or search online to find the books that most appeal to you. While the test is always the same, different authors take different approaches.

Online
Khan Academy is the Official SAT practice site. On their website, you

can find free, real, full-length SAT practice tests. You can also set up a personalized practice plan on their website that includes Official SAT Practice: www.khanacademy.org/sat.

The College Board also offers practice tests at www.collegereadiness.collegeboard.org/sat.

The website of the ACT offers their Official ACT study guide: www.act.org/.

REGISTERING FOR THE SAT

The College Board, the organization that owns the SAT, recommends that international students take the SAT within two years before they expect to start college.

You can register for the SAT in three ways: at the College Board's website online, by mail using the SAT paper registration form, or through an SAT representative.

According to the College Board website, online registration is not available to students in Benin, Cameroon, Ghana, Kenya, Nigeria, or Togo. In addition, there are specific identification requirements on the day of testing in these countries: Ghana, India, Nepal, Nigeria, Pakistan, Korea, Thailand, and Vietnam.

In China, the SAT is currently only given in schools authorized by the Ministry of Education. These are primarily international schools that enroll students who hold passports from countries outside of the People's Republic of China. Chinese national students who do not attend one of these schools and want to take the SAT can take it in SAT testing centers in Hong Kong, Macao, or any country outside of mainland China.

Registering Through an SAT International Representative
SAT International Representatives, also known as international service

providers, help students in their home countries with

- ▸ SAT registration
- ▸ In-language customer service
- ▸ Fee collection

IMPORTANT: Only use an authorized representative. You can find a list of authorized representatives for each county on the College Board website. Do a search on the College Board website for "SAT International Representatives" to find the list: www.collegeboard.org/

KNOW YOUR SAT AND ACT REPORTING RIGHTS

Most students have the opportunity to decide if their College Board (SAT) and their American College Testing (ACT) scores will be recorded on their transcripts. This will be done on an all-or-none basis.

If you do nothing, and your school has the capability to include scores, all scores (SAT, SAT Subject, and ACT tests) will be reported. If your choice is not to have your scores recorded on your transcripts, you can take advantage of the College Board Score Choice option, or even choose to send no scores. Please note that some schools don't accept the School Choice option, so check with each school individually on its policy.

Regardless of which option you choose, understand that all schools and some scholarships require official score reports from the testing agency.

In this case, the official score must be sent from the College Board or the American College Testing program.

SAT SUBJECT TESTS

SAT Subject Tests Overview
Many of the most competitive colleges, including the Ivies and various

top engineering programs, require or recommend that students take the SAT Subject Tests (formerly known as the SAT II and Achievement Tests). To them, these specific subject exams demonstrate your actual understanding of a subject area, meaning how well you have learned each subject and how prepared you will be for college-level courses.

Colleges often prefer the SAT Subject Tests because, like all standardized tests, they make the admissions department's job easier. For international students, SAT Subject Tests can be particularly useful, because colleges can easily use the test results to compare you to other students worldwide.

Colleges know that secondary school grades aren't always an accurate measurement of a student's ability. Some high schools are more difficult than others, some teachers are harder graders than others, and some students earn extra credit for random activities not available to all others. All of these possible factors leave equally talented students receiving different grades. Standardized tests are the great equalizer.

The tests include: Literature, U.S. History, World History, Mathematics Levels I and II, Biology, Chemistry, Physics, Computer Science, Chinese, French, German, Spanish, Modern Hebrew, Italian, Latin, Japanese, and Korean.

Not all schools require them, so you should check the universities' requirements before registering for any SAT Subject Tests. If you're not sure where you're going to apply, you should take at least two. If you're considering Georgetown, you should take three. Also, if a school "recommends" taking the Subject Test, you should. By taking the test, you are sending a message to the colleges about your interest in specific majors or programs.

The scores range from 200–800, much like the SAT. Colleges are generally happy with scores of 650 or above. Competitive schools want scores of 750 or more, depending on the subject. Make sure to focus on the tests you have a chance at doing well in. A poor score on an

SAT Subject Test may counteract a strong grade on your high school transcript in the same subject.

For international students, make sure you take the tests within two years before you expect to start college. If your chosen colleges ask for SAT Subject Tests, you'll need to register for these separately from your SAT registration. Also, be aware that SAT Subject Tests cannot be taken on the same day as the SAT.

Taking the SAT Subject Tests
Each exam is one hour in length. Prepare yourself as you would for the SAT. Get familiar with the format of the tests. Take old exams for practice if you can.

These tests aren't easy. The best time to take one of the SAT Subject Tests is right after you've finished a year-long course in that subject. This way the subject matter will still be fresh in your mind. Some exceptions would be if you plan to take the test in a Foreign Language or Literature. Then you'd want to take the test after the highest-level class you plan to take. Also, if you prefer a language exam with listening, be sure to check the date it is offered (normally in October). Obviously, there is no point in taking SAT Subject Tests after January of your last year of secondary school; everything should have been sent to the college admissions way before then. The only reason to take them this late would be if the colleges you're applying to use the SAT Subject Tests for placement or credit purposes.

The test dates for SAT Subject Tests are usually in August, October, November, December, January, May, and June. However, not every subject test is offered on each of the test dates. Note that you cannot take the SAT Subject Tests and the SAT on the same day, so you must plan your testing dates accordingly. To check when the tests you want to take are offered, refer to the College Board website at www.collegeboard.com.

Taking the SAT Subject Test in your native language

The foreign language tests are meant to demonstrate achievement in a language that was learned in school. If you have native fluency in a language, schools believe you would be better off taking an SAT Subject Test in a different language other than your native one. However, some native speakers take the test in their native language to waive foreign language requirements. If you do this, take another subject test, as well.

Registering for the SAT Subject Tests

Similar to registering for the SAT Test, international students can register for the SAT Subject Tests in three ways: at the College Board's website online, by mail using the SAT paper registration form, or through an SAT representative.

Online registration is not available to students in Benin, Cameroon, Ghana, Kenya, Nigeria, or Togo, and there are specific identification requirements on the day of testing in Ghana, India, Nepal, Nigeria, Pakistan, Korea, Thailand, and Vietnam.

Also, similar to the regular SAT Test, in China, SAT Subject Tests are currently only given in schools authorized by the Ministry of Education. Chinese students who do not attend one of these schools and want to take the SAT Subject Tests need to find another testing center by visiting the College Board website.

Registering Through an SAT International Representative

SAT International Representatives, also known as international service providers, can also help students with SAT Subject Test registration. Make sure to only use authorized representatives, who can be found on: www.collegeboard.org/.

INTERNATIONAL COLLEGE COUNSELORS TIP:

You can take up to three Subject Tests on the same day, but it's not recommended. We recommend two exams to one sitting. Don't underestimate the difficulty of these exams.

What do the SAT Subject Test scores mean?
An average score varies widely from test to test. It's all about who is taking the tests and what scores they earn. Most often, students aiming for highly competitive schools take the tests, because these are the schools that are asking for the scores.

What do the SAT Subject Test Scores mean to me?
The way to think about these scores is that they are part of your story. So, if you say you are great at math, you should do well on the math subject test. If you are just a "good" student with nothing really outstanding, these scores will likely support that.

TEST PREP COURSES

If you can take them, you should.

Some American high schools provide SAT/ACT prep courses as part of their curricular offerings.

Private tutors and private prep programs can teach you strategies tailored toward your learning level and ability. Furthermore, they offer the flexibility and convenience to work around your schedule and provide you with fewer distractions than class settings.

NO SAT OR ACT SCORES REQUIRED

There are some schools that don't use SAT or ACT scores for admitting students. Some of these schools only exempt students who meet certain grade point average (GPA) or class rank requirements. Other schools want to see your SAT or ACT scores, but only use them for placement purposes or to conduct research studies. If you are considering one of these schools, make sure you fully understand what the individual school's policy is. Admissions policies can and do change.

Here is a link to a list of SAT- and ACT-optional four-year colleges: www.fairtest.org/university/optional

New York University is an example of a school with extreme flexibility in accepting different scholastic exams for evaluating applicants. Along with either accepting the SAT or ACT, NYU also accepts three SAT Subject Tests, three AP exams, an IB Diploma, or three IB higher-level exams. They also accept other regional or national exams from dozens of countries around the world. If you did very well on any of these other exams, make sure to submit your best results instead of those from the SAT or ACT.

If a school does not require the SAT or ACT, be careful not to send them your scores. Some schools, like the University of Miami, will not overlook test scores received, even if they are not required.

ENGLISH LANGUAGE TESTS: TOEFL AND IELTS

If you are an international student from a non–English-speaking country who is interested in studying at an American university, you have probably heard about the TOEFL (Test of English as a Foreign Language) or IELTS (International English Language Testing System). These language assessment exams are offered in most of the world and accepted by nearly every university and scholarship program in the United States. The goals of the tests are to measure how well a student can use and understand English at the university level.

Both tests measure how well a person reads, listens, speaks, and writes in English, and how well they use these skills together. On the test, you may be asked to read a passage or listen to a lecture, and then write or speak about what you learned.

There are no passing or failing TOEFL or IELTS scores. Each school or scholarship sets its own score requirements. The most competitive colleges and programs typically expect a TOEFL Internet-based test score of 100 or higher or an IELTS score of 7. For some students it will be good to know that some schools do not require a TOEFL or IELTS score at all. However, without one of these scores you may need to attend English instructional sessions at the college before being accepted into regular academic courses.

TOEFL

There are two versions of the TOEFL test. The first is the iBT, or Internet-Based Test. The other is the TOEFL PBT Test, the Paper-Based Test. The vast majority of TOEFL test-takers worldwide take the Internet-based version of the test. Students are still able to take the TOEFL paper-based test, but it is being phased out.

The iBT and PBT have completely different structures. The iBT is given in English and administered only online. There are four sections (listening, reading, speaking, and writing). This takes a total of about four hours to complete. The iBT test includes questions to measure your ability to read, listen, and speak or write in response to a question. You also have to listen to someone speak and then speak in response to a question. In other words, the tasks are generally integrated with the listening, reading, and speaking mixed together.

The listening and speaking sections of the TOFEL iBT test now include other native-speaker English accents. In addition to accents from North America, you can hear accents from the United Kingdom, New Zealand, and Australia.

The Paper-Based Test takes about four hours to complete. There is also a thirty-minute writing test, called the TWE test. People who take the test will be measured on their abilities to write English, read English, and understand spoken English. The Paper-Based Test also has a section to test grammar, the rules governing the use of words and phrases. The Internet-Based Test does not.

To do well on the TOEFL, students should get to know the QWERTY keyboard, the standard keyboard used in America and the one used for the test. It is called a QWERTY keyboard because the top row of letters starts from the left with the letters *QWERTY*. As the exam is timed, you don't want to be spending extra time hunting for the correct letters if you are not familiar with the keyboard.

More information on the TOEFL and links to resources regarding this test can be found at www.ets.org/toefl.

IELTS

Similar to the TOEFL, the IELTS has four basic sections (reading, listening, speaking, and writing). Band scores are used for each language sub-skill and range from 0 ("Did not attempt the test") to 9 ("Expert user"). The IELTS is a significantly shorter exam—about two hours and forty-five minutes long, but don't mistake it as easier. Another big difference between the two tests is that on the IELTS test you will talk to a real person who will perform a one-on-one interview, whereas in the TOEFL test you will speak to a computer.

A variety of accents and writing styles have been presented in test materials, and so students should be able to understand a variety of dialects to do well. The IELTS test is a handwritten test, so it is critical for test-takers to have good handwriting or it may result in lower scores.

More information on the IELTS and links to resources concerning this test can be found at www.ielts.org.

TOEFL AND IELTS TIPS

Here are some tips for getting started with the TOEFL or IELTS:

Plan ahead.
Give yourself time to prepare for the test. Get to know the structure of the test and the kind of questions that will be asked. Many students study just before the test. This is not a good idea. Getting a good score or raising your score will take months of hard work.

Master the basics first.

Many students study for the TOEFL or IELTS before they are ready to do well. You should have an upper-intermediate English level before you attempt the test. If you score below 500 on the PBT, 70 on the iBT, or 5 on the IELTS, study the basics for a few months and then take the test again.

Get help.

A study guide or tutor can help you get the score you need. With a book you can improve your reading, writing, and note-taking skills. A personal tutor can make sure your pronunciation is clear, as well as assess how you're doing in the speaking and writing sections. There are online practice tests on the official TOEFL and IELTS websites. The practice tests may be costly, but I always recommend using the official practice tests.

Use outside resources.

Make English part of your daily life. Listen to podcasts, talk with English speakers, watch movies, read newspapers and books, send and read text messages in English, and/or purchase digital audiobooks.

Learn how to write an English essay.

Both the TOEFL and IELTS tests require you to write an essay. In a short amount of time, you'll have to analyze the question, think of ideas to write about, plan an essay, and then write it. Practice writing this essay many times. Make sure you know how to write an essay with an introduction, a body of two to three supporting paragraphs, and a conclusion.

Take the test as many times as you need to practice.

Colleges will not know your TOEFL or IELTS scores unless you send the scores to them. The college will also not know how many times you took the test unless you report this information.

One thing to note is that scores on both exams expire two years after the test date. The best way to score high on the TOEFL or IELTS is to know how to read, write, and speak English well.

CLEP (College-Level Examination Program)

The CLEP allows students to get college credit by taking an examination. These exams test undergraduate-level knowledge in specific subjects. Doing well on a CLEP exam can earn you the same amount of college credit as if you took and passed a college course. International students can bypass certain introductory undergraduate courses by taking the CLEP.

Unlike the tests previously mentioned, these exams are not required for admission to U.S. colleges and universities. Passing a CLEP exam offers specific benefits for international students, including:

Credit for language skills
International students can earn undergraduate credit and fulfill foreign language requirements. Language tests are offered in Spanish, French, and German.

Credit for previous study
When students have earned credit at an international college or university that is not transferable to a U.S. school, CLEP exams can provide an alternate way for students to demonstrate that they know the college-level material.

By testing out of courses, students can earn a degree more quickly and save money on tuition and fees.

TAKING A CLEP EXAM

CLEP exams are accepted by 2,900 colleges and universities. The exams are computer-based and are administered at 1,400 test centers. Most of the test centers are in the United States. There are a few international CLEP test centers, but not many. For this reason, we encourage international students to take CLEP exams once they arrive at a U.S. school.

Before taking the CLEP exams, students should talk to their international student advisors or the admissions office to know which CLEP exams are recognized by their chosen college.

The website for the CLEP exams is https://clep.collegeboard.org/.

Chapter 8

AP and IB Courses and Tests

I f you're a strong student, you should take the most advanced classes you can. This often means taking Advanced Placement (AP) or International Baccalaureate (IB) courses.

Colleges prefer that you take these courses, and they're good for you. Both are good and show that you've challenged yourself academically. Students in the United Kingdom or at a British school should consider taking the General Certificate of Education Advanced Level courses, more commonly known as A-Levels, which I'll also discuss in this chapter.

AP COURSES

AP courses are designed to give you college-level courses in high school. Through AP exams, you can earn college credits and gain significant advantages in the college admissions process and while applying to scholarships. (See chapter 19 on how they can even save you money.)

AP courses are offered in more than one hundred countries. International schools and American-style schools outside of the United States offer the AP program. It is also offered by a number of schools that are part of various countries' national school systems. Additionally, AP courses can be found online through a variety of virtual school options.

Currently, there are over thirty-five AP courses to choose from, including Art History, Chemistry, Computer Science, Environmental Science, European History, Music Theory, Physics, Psychology, Statistics, Studio Art Drawing, and World History.

The final exam score is reported on a scale of 1–5 (1 being the lowest, and 5 being the highest), and it shows how well you mastered the material.

Most four-year colleges in the United States give credit, accelerated placement, or both on the basis of AP exam scores. By entering college with AP credits, you can save money on college courses and possibly even graduate from college early.

Whether you receive the college credits depends on your scores and on your college. All colleges set their own standards. Most colleges will give college credit for a score of 3, while the more highly selective colleges require a score of 4 or higher. A few of the Ivies, like Harvard and Yale, use the credit toward programs like Advanced Standing Program or Acceleration Credit. Check each school's policy regarding exam results. Additionally, some schools limit how many AP credits they will accept regardless of your scores.

There is no right or wrong number of AP courses to take. These are considered in the context of the rest of your application.

If you are applying to the more competitive schools, I recommend that you take as many AP classes as you can handle.

Students who are pursuing university study outside of their native country should consider applying for the AP International Diploma (APID), a globally recognized award. The APID requires a score of 3 or higher on five AP exams. It provides additional certification of academic excellence.

TO REPORT THE AP TEST OR NOT TO REPORT THE AP TEST?

After taking one of the many various AP tests, there are usually three ways a student will feel: Great! Good. Or bad.

If you think you did "great" or "good," congratulations!

If you're sure you did badly and you scored a 1 or a 2, or if you're not sure how you did but you have a sick feeling in your stomach about your performance, you can withhold or even cancel your score.

Schools do not ask you to send official scores any more with the applications, so you are usually free to let the college know your scores only if you want. Of course, if you list that you took an AP class, but you don't disclose a score, the most competitive colleges will assume that you got a 1 or a 2. Therefore, if you did get a 1 or 2, I would recommend leaving it off altogether.

Many public colleges do not request AP scores on applications, so you do not need to worry. They are requested on the Common Application, but not required.

Because AP scores are released in July, any request for changes in reporting must be received by June 15.

Note that it's not likely that any one AP score you submit, no matter how low, will harm your chances for general admission. However, if you are trying to get into a top undergraduate engineering program, and you score a 1 on the AP Calculus AB exam, colleges will not see this as good.

CANCELING AP SCORES

Canceling an AP score permanently means that you will not see the score and it will be deleted from your record forever.

However, colleges will likely know that you took the test because the class will still appear on your transcript.

The option to cancel a score helps a number of students. Some of those students took an AP course but found they didn't learn all the information that was covered on the test. (This actually happens more often than you'd think.) This option also encourages the risk-takers, the students who take an AP exam in a subject in which they might not have taken a class.

To cancel a score, you must notify the College Board by sending them an AP Score Cancellation Form by mail or by fax with your signature by the middle of June. (The date may change, so visit www.apscore.org for the most updated information.)

The service to cancel a score is free, but be aware that the score report that you and your school receive will show that the score has been canceled.

INTERNATIONAL COLLEGE COUNSELORS TIP:
Do not designate colleges to send your AP scores to on your answer sheet. Wait until you have seen your scores to decide when and which colleges to send them to.

TAKE THE AP TEST WITHOUT TAKING AN AP COURSE

Very few schools offer all AP courses. Many international schools don't offer AP courses at all. Some students find that the AP course they want doesn't fit into their schedule. What if you are one of these students?

Colleges understand that not everyone has access to AP courses. You can still take the AP tests if you want to, whether you're an international student, have been homeschooled, have attended an unaccredited private school, or reside in a school or city with few options.

If your school already offers AP courses:
Contact your school's AP coordinator to register for any of the exams, whether your school offers the course or not. He or she will guide you through the registration process.

If you attend a school that does not offer AP courses:

If you attend a school that does not offer AP courses, you may need to study on your own, take the course at another school, or take an online course. Then you will need to arrange to take the test at a testing center near you. Students who want to take an AP exam should contact AP Services at +1 212 632 1780, or at apexams@info.collegeboard.org. For more information on registering for AP Exams, visit the College Board international students page at:
https://international.collegeboard.org/prepare-to-study-in-the-us.

To find which schools offer AP courses in your country, check the AP Course Ledger at https://apcourseaudit.epiconline.org/ledger/ and begin your search by entering your country in the "Ledger Search" area. The AP Course Ledger is the official record of schools that offer authorized courses. Courses that are not listed on the AP Course Ledger are not recognized by universities as AP courses.

The College Board has specific web pages for AP courses and exams for students in Canada, China, and India:
http://international.collegeboard.org/programs/advanced-placement.

AP TEST PREPARATION

To prepare for the AP exams, use standard study books from trustworthy sources, like the Princeton Review and the College Board.

Students without access to AP courses in their high school may consider courses offered by local institutions and private companies. Some universities, such as Stanford and the University of California, offer online learning programs that include AP courses.

When researching your options, make sure that the AP course is approved by the College Board. The College Board maintains strict curriculum standards for AP courses. Also, you need to check with your secondary school to see whether or not it will give you credit for taking the course.

IB COURSES

Similar to AP courses, the International Baccalaureate (IB) program is a high school program that offers college-level courses, the opportunity to earn college credits, and the ability to gain advantages in the college admissions process.

IB is offered in nearly 4,000 IB schools in close to 150 countries. To earn the diploma, you have to take a certain number of courses in a varying range of subjects. You can take a few IBs without actually earning the diploma, but IB was developed to be a set program of courses.

Over the course of the two-year IB Diploma Program, students follow a curriculum that is made up of the Diploma Program (DP) core and six subject groups. The three DP core elements are: Theory of Knowledge (TOK); the Extended Essay; and Creativity, Activity, and Service (CAS). Students study six subjects chosen from the six subject groups, and the schools select the DP subject courses it will offer to students. The six subject groups include: studies in language; studies in literature; language acquisition; sciences; mathematics; and the arts.

Students may take some subjects at the higher level (HL) and some at the standard level (SL). Each student takes at least three (but not more than four) subjects at the higher level, and the remaining at the standard level.

While the AP program focuses on multiple-choice exams, the IB emphasizes writing. A long, college-style research paper is required of all IB diploma students. IB also has extracurricular requirements.

Students must be enrolled in an IB class to take an IB exam.

IB DIPLOMA PROGRAM

To earn an IB diploma, you must take at least three higher-level courses. Most colleges give credit for higher-level IB exams, but not all give credit for standard-level IB exams. Many colleges often use a score of 4 or 5 as the minimum for granting credit. Highly selective colleges only accept scores of 5 or higher on a language exam or 6 or higher in other subjects.

For the full Diploma Program, which is different than an individual DP course score, the minimum passing score is 24 points, assuming that all other passing conditions have been met. The highest total score available for a Diploma Program student is 45 points.

Similar to the AP exams, schools like Harvard and Yale apply IB credits to their Advanced Standing Program or accept the scores only as Acceleration Credits. To look up any college's IB credit policy, you should do an online search for "[Name of College/University] IB credit."

RETAKING IB EXAMS

If you are not satisfied with the grade you have achieved in a subject, or for the theory of knowledge or extended essay requirement, you may take the subject(s) again. This can be in the examination session provided six months later or after any period of time.

Students may retake exams a maximum of two times. Diploma candidates have a maximum of three examination sessions in which to obtain their diploma. When retaking a session, the next session will have another syllabus, so you would also have to comply with any new requirements.

REPORTING IB RESULTS

Most decisions regarding admission are made before the announcement of the results of IB exams. This means that many universities request that the student's high school sends the university predicted grades in the different subjects, as well as the theory of knowledge and extended essay. Universities will use these predicted grades to make admissions decisions.

Before IB results are released, you can request to have results sent to one U.S. university for free. All requests must be submitted by your school's IB program coordinator. Additional transcript requests can be made for a fee of US $17 per U.S. university.

IB TEST PREPARATION

The best way to study for the IB exams is to take practice exams from the official testing material. Students should ask teachers for exams from the years before or buy curriculum and assessment materials from the IB store found at www.follettibstore.com. Students may also watch instructional videos on YouTube or hire a personal tutor for more help.

A-LEVELS

The General Certificate of Education Advanced Level (A-Levels) is a school-leaving qualification offered by educational bodies in the United Kingdom and other British Crown dependencies, including India, Singapore, Pakistan, and Malaysia. Similar to AP and IB courses, they are highly valued by universities.

A-Levels are generally worked toward over two years and split into two parts, with one part studied in each year. The first part is known as the Advanced Subsidiary Level, or AS Level. AS Levels can be taken as a stand-alone qualification, or as the first part of an A-Level course. AS Levels are completed at the end of Year 12. The second part is known as the A2 Level, which is taken at the end of Year 13. The AS Level combined with the A2 Level form the complete A-Level qualification.

Students usually take four subjects in Year 12. After the AS Level exams, they drop one subject and continue the other three through Year 13 to complete A-Levels.

AS Levels and A-Levels are mostly assessed by written exams, although there is also some coursework available in most subjects. In subjects like science and art, a student's practical skills are also assessed.

AS and A-Levels are graded from A*–E, A* being the highest and E being the lowest. Your report will also show a score on the Uniform Mark Scale (UMS). This is a mark out of 300 at AS and out of 600 at A-Level. If you're not happy with a score, you can retake a unit. At this time, A-Levels can now only be retaken in the summer, usually in the month of June.

To receive final credit for your A-Levels, you must present your official A-Level certificate. Different universities have different policies about what they will accept for this credit. Several universities require a minimum passing grade of C for AS-Level and A-Level courses, while some of the more highly competitive schools accept only A*, A, or possibly B scores. Other schools do not accept A-Levels for credit at all, so make sure to check with each respective university about their policies.

OTHER SCHOLASTIC EXAMS

There are dozens of other nationally accredited exams. Although most U.S. universities only accept AP, IB, and possibly A-Levels, some colleges will accept scores from provincial, national, or other board exams. You should review each university's website or contact the university to see which exams they will accept, what their minimum scores are, and what you must provide as documentation.

Chapter 9

Summer Opportunities

Make summer count. Students who want to shine on their college applications must make the most of their summers.

Below is a variety of ideas on how you can maximize your summer vacation periods:

Get a great summer job or internship.
Summer jobs and internships are great ways to show colleges—and your parents—that you are successfully maturing into a responsible adult. There are few better ways to earn both respect and valuable real-world experience.

If jobs in your area are hard to find, your best option may be an internship. You will get paid very little or not at all; that's what "internship" means. However, you will become rich in experience and résumé fodder. Think of it as an actual summer course.

Your best-case scenario is to land an internship in a field in which you are interested in pursuing. This will be your chance to try out a job before you choose to major in that field of study. If you think you might like to pursue a career in advertising, check with your local media agencies to see what internship opportunities are available. If you hope to be a lawyer, see if you can work in a law firm for the summer. An internship is also great way to secure a good recommendation and get your foot in the door for future networking.

Having a summer internship or job can also help you narrow down what you *don't* like.

Take a job as a salesperson, and maybe you'll find that you hate having to deal with people's inquiries or complaints. Work in an office, and perhaps you'll discover that the job is too boring for you. Working with an architect or at a television station might strip away the glamorous façade of the career and show you what the day-to-day experience at that type of job can really be like.

More information and tips on jobs and interviews can be found in chapter 10.

Volunteer.
Working for nothing can actually be profitable to you. You can make a difference, gain experience, and explore your interests. For example, if a career in medicine interests you, you could volunteer a few hours a week at a hospital or nursing home. Interested in animals? Volunteer at the local animal shelter. Feeling entrepreneurial? Start a nonprofit of your own. The choices are endless, and all your hard work and time spent volunteering can really pay off. Colleges and universities prefer students who can demonstrate that they make the effort to help others. You might not be making money, but you can make friends and networking connections. You'll also be accruing valuable material for those application essays and increasing your chances of winning a financial scholarship. Then there's the ultimate bottom line: You will be doing good—a wonderful reason to volunteer in and of itself.

Take a virtual class.
Enhance your résumé and explore something new. Virtual or online classes offer you a chance to choose something you want to learn about. Try out a course from a major in which you're interested. Explore aeronautical science or 17th century literature. Taking such courses demonstrates intellectual curiosity to a college. These courses can also serve as good practice for the TOEFL or IELTS test.

Pre-College Summer Programs
At a pre-college summer program, you can grow your mind, strengthen

your college application, and explore possible fields of study. You can also get a chance to spend some time in the United States on a college campus. Pre-college summer programs also offer marvelous opportunities to make contact with students, professors, and administrators for advice, guidance, and letters of recommendation.

Pre-college summer program offerings include art, computer science, engineering, physics, biomedical engineering, theater, and more. Actually, for any interest, there is likely a pre-college summer program somewhere. There are summer programs focused on community service, health care, language, cultural immersion . . . the list could go on and on.

Programs generally range in length from one to six weeks. Some of these programs can even allow you to earn college credit. Depending on the college you attend, you may be able to transfer the credits over to the school.

Some programs are highly competitive, and others are open to anyone who can pay the fees. Many of these programs are expensive, but some do offer scholarships. I generally recommend these types of programs to students who have a strong interest in a particular subject and who can afford the program.

Dive into a language immersion program.
There are a number of programs available both in the United States and abroad. Perfecting a second or third language is always beneficial. If you want to study in the United States, perfecting your English is extremely worthwhile. There are a number of colleges and universities in the United States that offer summer TOEFL and test preparation programs. Additional benefits of studying in the United States in a summer program are cultural immersion and a greater understanding of the country. If you already speak English well, consider a language immersion program in a third language. Due to the growing emphasis on a global education, colleges look more and more favorably on

students who can speak more than one or even two languages.

Start a business.
Launching a business or collaborating on one can be a great learning experience that can provide students with valuable skills—and income. The general recommendation is that students start a simple business with an immediate and obvious customer base. The goal is to generate a profit. Students with a passion for business who want to learn more about entrepreneurship may consider attending a program to help them get started. Nova Southeastern University in Florida, for example, offers a program called the Entrepreneurship Summer Camp and Personal Enrichment (ESCAPE) program. There are a number of similar programs around the United States.

SUMMER IMPACT ON SCHOLARSHIPS

I will talk about this more in chapter 20, but certain scholarships are available for students who show a high interest in pursuing certain careers. By using the summer break to take a qualifying interest to a higher level, you may become eligible for these scholarships. Demonstrating long-term interest in certain volunteer work or organizations can also boost your scholarship chances. Taking classes at a local community college or school can show colleges a deep interest in a particular scholarly area that may make you eligible for scholarships at their school.

As you weigh your options, know that colleges are looking for any experience you are gaining that is helping to guide you toward your long-term goals.

Highly selective colleges also judge the quality of your experiences. To maximize the impact of a summer program, internship, volunteer position, or job on your application, I recommend that you choose one that is part of an overall plan or strategy. Make sure that any summer activities you choose help to show you as a person who is passionate about particular subjects or services.

For example, if your focus has been on art, spending time in Italy studying art makes sense. If you choose a summer community service program, find a way to build on that experience when you return home. If you helped supervise an art camp for young children in Guatemala and saw that they needed more art supplies, perhaps you could start a fund-raising organization for them or seek donations to send back to the art camp. Enjoy your summer—wisely!

Chapter 10

Jobs and Internships

S ummer jobs and internships (whether they're paid or not) are a great way to prepare for life after high school or for college. These experiences can help you develop the professional talents you'll need at almost any job. This is an opportunity to work with diverse people in a professional setting; hone your time management skills; develop your real-world problem-solving techniques; learn to follow instructions; and be allowed the freedom to make mistakes that won't hurt your career. Jobs and internships are also excellent boosters of self-esteem and self-confidence. If you can succeed in one job, you realize that you can succeed in many others.

HOW TO FIND AN INTERNSHIP OR JOB THAT IS RIGHT FOR YOU

To find an internship or job that will suit your needs, use a combination of strategies.

Start looking early.
Start your internship/job search during the winter break. Finding an internship or job may be as easy as searching the web—a number of them are posted on websites. Other opportunities may require more effort or creativity to find.

Know what interests you.
Begin with an idea of what you want to do. While you're not expected to commit to any specific field during an internship, colleges want to see that you've used some kind of educated strategy in choosing your jobs or internships. Is there something you want to learn how to do, or a goal you want to reach in ten years? Start with your interests. This is your chance to try out a career. Are you considering a major in business, psychology, or political science? Are you interested in computers, sports, or animals?

management"

Search the Internet.
Think about what kind of job you want, then look up employers in your area for whom you think you'd want to work. Check the company websites. They may have an internship or job posted already. If not, call or email them and inquire about summer jobs or internships. Be prepared to give a short discussion of your skills, strengths, and reasons for hoping to work there.

Start with the front desk person and then do a search to see if the company has someone "higher up" who can help you.

Network, network, and network some more.
Speak with family members, friends, your family's friends, teachers, and school advisors about what type of job or internship you might want to pursue. Ask if they have any connections in the field. Maybe they can help you connect with possible employers or know someone who can. You will not know until you ask. Send a thank-you note to anyone who helps you. Express your appreciation for their time and expertise.

Join LinkedIn.
LinkedIn enables you to find people you know or want to know and connect with them. You can ask your connections about job opportunities, join more specific job-related groups, and be informed of job opportunities. If you do decide to contact someone you do not know, send a brief explanation of who you are and why you want to connect with them.

Do it the old-fashioned way.
Fill out applications or drop off résumés at prospective employers' offices and temporary employment agencies.

Be creative.
Email or call someone in a company whose work you admire. Flatter them and then see if they might need a helper or an assistant. The worst they can do is say no. Even if the person you call does say no, write them a short note thanking them for their time and providing them with your contact information, but then do not call again.

If you can't find the job you want, think about creating your own.

Don't limit yourself.
A job or internship should primarily be about learning, unless you need the money. When you have the option to take an unpaid internship or a lower-paying job, you will obviously have more choices. If you are financially able to work for free, or volunteer, you may be able to create your own position at a family member's or friend's company. You may be able to get a job or an internship at a company where you really want to work if you're willing to start out working for free. You are in essence exchanging receiving low or no pay for invaluable work experience that helps to build your résumé.

Make your own luck.
You may "get lucky" on your very first call, but most likely you won't. This is a numbers game—the more people you call, the luckier you will get. Think positively, and do not give up. You may get the job you want after one call, or after fifty. Your biggest mistake here will be not trying hard enough.

Stay safe.
Keep your parent, guardian, or another responsible adult informed of your job and internship search. If you decide to apply for a position, especially one you have discovered online, first tell an adult you trust. Never go for an in-person interview without letting an adult know where you will be.

THE JOB OR INTERNSHIP INTERVIEW

Normally, interviewers of high school students aren't looking for previous work history or unique skills. They simply want someone who is smart, organized, a good communicator, and a good fit for the company. Both your attitude and your appearance will affect your chances of getting the job you want.

Here are a few things to remember:

Dress the part.
When you head out for your interview, avoid looking too casual. That means no sandals, jeans, sunglasses, or hats. Even if you will be scooping ice cream behind a counter, it still helps to look professional for the interview. See chapter 6 for tips on what to wear to an interview.

Do your research.
Before the interview, go online and learn everything you can about the business with which you'll be interviewing, including its corporate mission statement (a declaration of the company's purpose and what it's trying to achieve), its products or services, and what customers are saying about it. Then use what you learn when answering the interviewer's questions. You can also go onto their Twitter, Facebook, or Instagram accounts to glean the latest company information.

Be polite and professional.
Send a thank-you note after the interview.

HOW TO MAKE THE MOST OF YOUR SUMMER INTERNSHIP OR JOB

Turn your experience into résumé gold.
Find an internship or a job in a field in which you are interested. However, any job or internship can ultimately lead to great opportunities. Volunteer for extra tasks and look for opportunities to demonstrate your initiative and skills. The best first step is to prove that you're responsible and resourceful.

For example, if you're working in an ice cream shop and your boss needs to leave a few hours early, volunteer to be put in charge. If you're given the responsibility to lead, this can count on your résumé as "management skills." If you're working in an advertising firm and think you might want to become an advertising copywriter, ask for a few current assignments. Write the ads, then ask for feedback. The company might love your ad so much, they'll run it.

Make connections.
Build up personal relationships. Find a mentor. After the summer is over, stay in touch with the people you met and connected with—and stay connected. It's never too early to start building your professional network. As previously mentioned, a social networking site like LinkedIn is a good place to keep in touch.

Develop your professional "people skills."
Hone in on people whom you admire. Study the qualities you admire in them. Take notes on how they dress and what character traits have put them ahead. Then try to emulate those traits.

Work on your professionalism.
Do what you can to show the company that you're the one they should be watching and to whom they should be giving the best assignments. Be professional, serious about your tasks, and responsible. This should earn you more respect and responsibility. Be on time for work, meetings, conference calls, and team-building exercises. Make sure you dress for success.

Be proactive.
If your job or internship has you doing jobs like making photocopies or brewing the coffee, don't complain. Perform these tasks to the best of your ability, and then request a meeting with your supervisor to ask about new opportunities or projects. If there is a task you would like to try, ask your supervisor if you can join that particular team, observe their meetings, or otherwise contribute in some way. You won't know unless you ask. Even if they say no, you will gain the respect and attention of your older colleagues. Interns and employees who identify their employer's needs and ask for new challenges demonstrate the initiative and motivation that companies ultimately want.

Ask questions.
Always remember that a summer job or internship is a learning experience

103

for you. While your employer expects to get some productive work from you, you are also expected to be interested in what's going on. So ask questions. This is your chance to get advice and learn.

Learn to take criticism gracefully.

No one likes to be criticized, but you're sure to encounter many negative opinions throughout your life and your career. Criticism can actually help you if you keep a good attitude. Follow up a negative review by asking for the person's thoughts on what you could have done better. Are there resources you don't know about? Is it true that you need to be more detail-oriented? Then put that information to good use. The best part about a summer job or internship is that you're not expected to know everything yet. Both you and your employer know that you are there to learn.

Learn about yourself.

You're there to watch and observe. Use this time to find out more about yourself. See what kind of people you relate to best and what kind of work you like to do. Compare yourself to people on the job whom you admire. Do they have skills you lack or can work on acquiring?

Reset your expectations.

It's good to have personal goals, but sometimes reality doesn't match our expectations. Rather than dwell on the negative aspects of the job or internship, seek out and embrace the opportunities that it offers. Chances are, you won't be given the assignment that saves a client and makes you a star. But that's not why you're there at this time. You're there to learn, to expand your horizons, and to build up your résumé. And always, always stay enthusiastic and positive!

A JOB OR INTERNSHIP FROM THE COLLEGE'S POINT OF VIEW

Did you know that a challenging and educational internship that gives you practical, real-life experience can look as good as or even better on your college application as attending a fancy, expensive pre-college program?

The trend for competitive, affluent, college-bound students several years ago was doing volunteer work—the more exotic, the better. But then the experience of "taking two weeks out of the summer to help malaria victims in East Africa" started to appear on many college applications.

So admission officers began to look for something more authentic to set students apart from one another. The result has been that many college applications now ask for your "paid employment" experiences.

Interesting, as well, is that admissions officers at several elite schools say they are giving *more* credit to students who have real-world jobs and *less* credit to students who have taken on short-term activities that do not show that student's passions. For community service to really count on your application, you need to show a solid pattern of continual volunteer activity in an area of real passion and interest to you.

In addition, I have worked with many Ivy League–bound students who have worked as cleaners, landscapers, and waiters. These jobs show commitment and the ability to work hard, and chances are that the parents of these students did not secure them these jobs. Such paid positions demonstrate the students' ability and initiative to pursue and secure a job on their own—showing responsibility, passion, and determination.

Now is the time to start thinking about the future, not just college, but beyond. Just as important as the question of which college to attend is the question of what you want to do. If you have fallen in love with the field of agricultural science or primatology, attending the Harvard summer program in physics or creative writing probably will not help you in such a career.

Getting real-life work experience will demonstrate those things in which you are interested, careers in which you want to become involved, and activities about which you are passionate.

INTERNATIONAL COLLEGE COUNSELORS TIP:
The trick to filling in the employment section of your high school résumé is to look for opportunities in which you will be given the chance to actually *do* something. Don't worry about the name of the company; look at the job itself when choosing among your options.

Chapter 11

Volunteering and Community Service

COMMUNITY SERVICE PROJECTS THAT MAKE AN IMPACT

There are many reasons to do volunteer work:

- It's a requirement for graduation from certain high schools.
- It will put you in a better position to get certain scholarships.
- You may get high school credit and/or graduation recognition.
- U.S. colleges have come to expect it.
- Volunteer work looks great on a college application.
- Volunteer work provides great topics for college essays.
- You have the opportunity to explore different career options.
- You may become passionate about a cause.
- It feels good to do good for others.

You can find volunteer opportunities through clubs, schools, religious institutions, family members, friends, or on your own.

The Perfect Community Service Combo: Passion, Commitment, Dedication, and Initiative
The applicant who will get the most attention from colleges is not the one who claims, "I volunteered four hundred hours in one year." What will capture the college admissions officer's attention is how you talk about what you did and what you can say about it.

Ideally you want to be able to say something like, "I volunteered at an economically disadvantaged school, where I started a music program for low-income children, raised funds to support it, recruited and trained more volunteers for the program, secured the donation of the instruments, and gained community recognition for the project in the local paper."

In the above statement, the student shows passion, leadership, commitment, dedication, and initiative.

Best of the best is if you earn a position of leadership with a title. Best of the best of the best is if you get public recognition for your service. Perhaps you can appear in your local or school paper or—best of the best of the best of the best—get a national publication to take notice of you.

Colleges like when you choose a volunteer opportunity that is consistent with your educational or career goals. If you're interested in going to medical school, volunteer in a hospital or with children with disabilities. If you want to be a lawyer, try working on an environmental campaign. If you have good public relations skills, consider organizing fund-raisers for good causes. If you like to cook, help feed poor people. Find something you enjoy doing, and you'll have no trouble earning the hours.

Volunteer doing something you love, and it won't feel like work. Of course, the worst of the worst is doing no volunteer work at all.

HOW TO ACHIEVE THAT PERFECT COMMUNITY SERVICE COMBO

Clock the time.
You can work 100 hours a year. You can work 1,000 hours a year. Interestingly, the number of hours you volunteer is not the most important factor. Colleges want to know *why* you volunteered, *how* you chose the assignment, and *how* you handled your responsibilities.

Hours are important for you to show a pattern of consistency. On many applications, including the Common Application, you must write hours per week/weeks per year.

Demonstrate focus.
It's better to be really involved in one or two volunteer activities than do a few hours here and there or spend your time on lots of little meaningless projects.

If you spent a short period of time helping out with a project abroad, you need to turn that experience into a long-term mission once you return home. Unless you plan on going into Latin American Studies or Construction Management, colleges prefer you spend four years helping at a local shelter than spending a month building houses in Guatemala, unless you are from Guatemala.

The ultimate goal is for you to become part of something important and show that you made an impact. A college wants to know that you found a focus.

Think creatively.
Think about ways you can expand on your community service. Come up with a goal of your own. If you are tutoring kids, make it a project to recruit more tutors. If you're working with the elderly, see if you can get a group of students to entertain them once a month. If you work with rescue animals, make cute videos encouraging people to adopt.

Areas of Community Service to Consider (with examples)

‣ Children (Do volunteer work at a local school or youth center.)

‣ Animals (Work at an animal rescue.)

‣ Elderly (Aid in a nursing home.)

‣ Tutoring (Assist middle school students with their homework.)

‣ Office work (Do social media work for a nonprofit group.)

‣ Environment (Clean a community park.)

‣ Hunger, housing, and homelessness (Serve food at a homeless shelter.)

- ▸ Medical (Participate in a hospital volunteer program.)

- ▸ Computer science (Create a website or community forum for a nonprofit.)

- ▸ Retail (Work at a local charity shop or thrift store run by a charitable organization.)

The Service Trip Trap

Many companies offer exotic international trips with community service attachments. Before paying the thousands of dollars to attend, know that admissions officers are not very impressed with these trips. More and more students have been traveling abroad to fulfill community service requirements, and it is no longer seen as a unique accomplishment. If you do go on one of these trips, make sure you also volunteer locally and find a way to expand on your experience. No matter where you do your community service, the main importance is to demonstrate focus, commitment, dedication, and initiative.

Of course, if you have the opportunity to go, can afford the trip, and do more volunteer work at home, go; it is a great experience to go on a service trip. For students who can't afford the program cost, which typically runs US $5,000 to US $7,000 and more, some programs offer financial aid and outreach programs.

IF YOU CAN'T VOLUNTEER

There are exceptions to every "rule." If you truly can't afford to volunteer since you may need to watch a younger sibling or work to help support your family, make sure you explain this situation in your essay or in the "additional information" section on the application. If you explain your economic situation and how you are helping your family, a number of admissions officers will consider this a form of service.

INTERNATIONAL COLLEGE COUNSELORS TIP:
When describing your volunteer work/community service in your college admissions essays, make sure that you let the reader know what your experiences have taught you.

Chapter 12

Demonstrating Interest

Colleges want to know you're interested in them. In fact, they want you more if they think you want them. Colleges do not want to admit students who are not serious about them.

There is a reason for this. The percent of admitted students who actually join the freshman class is important to college rankings. If a student is accepted and then rejects the college, this can bring down the college's points and ranking. When you show interest, a college believes you are more likely to accept their offer of admission.

Students need to show interest in the colleges to which they are applying. By showing interest, students are letting the college know that it is important to them.

Here are ideas you can use to demonstrate the kind of interest colleges like to see:

Visits
Visiting a campus is the best way to see if you like a school. Campus visits are also one of the best ways to show a college that you are interested in it. However, colleges understand that some students live too far away to make a visit possible. If you are far away, you will not be penalized. A number of colleges offer "virtual tours." Take a look at these if they are offered. Some schools also offer fly-in programs or travel stipends for prospective applicants or admitted students. If you want to visit a college and need help, call the admissions office and inquire about financial support for visits. Read more about college tours and visits in chapter 13.

Information requests
Requesting information and getting on a college's mail/email list shows

a college you are interested. Plus, this is good for you. You receive printed materials and emails that allow you to get to know the school. You may also receive invitations to campus or local events.

Online information forms
Create an online admissions profile with the colleges you are interested in, if they offer this. You will gain access to a web portal that provides information and services from the school. You may also be able to submit and track your online application, schedule a campus tour, and interact with college representatives.

Open emails
If a college sends you an email, open it. A college can see whether or not you opened your email. Colleges can also see whether or not you clicked on the links in the email. So click some links!

Research
Know something about the school and program you are interested in before visiting a campus or meeting with an admissions representative. You want to know enough to ask intelligent questions and have a good discussion. You do not want to ask any questions that can be found on the web or in the printed materials.

Local events
If a college event or college fair is scheduled within reasonable distance of your home, attend it. Go to the tables of the schools you are interested in and sign in. You will be entered in the college database as someone who is interested. Use the same name that you will use on your applications. Introduce yourself to the representative and get their contact information. When you get home, write the representative a thank-you note for their time and information. (See below: Saying thanks.)

School presentations
If a college representative visits your school, attend the presentation. They've traveled far to see you and they appreciate the audience. Visit

your guidance office to find out upcoming dates and times well in advance of these visits. If you don't have a guidance office at your high school, you can also call the college to see if a representative will visit.

Social media

More and more admissions staff use social media tools like Facebook, Twitter, Instagram, blogs, and online chats to communicate with prospective students. Engaging colleges through the use of social media is a great way to demonstrate interest. Make sure your personal pages are ones you would want a college to see.

Interviews

Schedule an interview with an admissions representative, if possible, unless your English skills are not good. Interviews offer you the opportunity to learn more while expressing your interest in the campus, community, programs, and activities offered by a college. Interviews can take place on campus with an admissions representative, in your community with a local alum, or via Skype. Read more about interviewing in chapter 6.

Essays

Here's a secret: Colleges *really care* about the specific supplemental essay questions they append to shared application forms. Take the time to show knowledge of the college by tailoring your responses based on details of programs and campus life you've gleaned from visits, written materials, or interacting on the social network. The more specific, the better, even if it means creating different personal statements with shout-outs to your favorite colleges.

Correspondence

Respond to all emails or letters that ask for a response. If you have a question, try to write or call someone you met in admissions or your area representative. If you have not met anyone, check the college website to see who is in the Office of Admissions that you can call. If the information is not available on the website, call the admissions office to find out the name and email address of an admissions

114

representative to contact. Make sure your correspondence or calls are short and direct. Make sure you check your spelling and grammar.

Participate in online chats hosted by the college

A number of schools host online chats for prospective students. These chats usually give you chance to ask questions to admissions officers and current students.

Faculty and staff contacts

If you meet a member of the faculty or staff of a program or major that interests you, keep in touch with that person. Your connection may be good to mention or describe in a college essay. The person you know may even help you with admissions.

Saying thanks

After you meet with any admissions representative or attend an interview, take the time to follow up with a short thank-you note. This can be either handwritten or sent by email. See how to write a thank-you note in chapter 13.

Early applications

Students who apply Early Decision (ED) or Early Action (EA) show a college that they are really interested. Make sure to apply before the deadline. If a school offers a priority or rolling application deadline, submit your application as soon as possible. For more information on applying early, see chapter 2.

INTERNATIONAL COLLEGE COUNSELORS TIP:

Demonstrating interest does not mean you should harass colleges and admissions staff. Use good judgment and be strategic. Also, you, not your parent, should be the one contacting the college. By calling directly and not having your parent do it, you're demonstrating maturity, independence, and interest—all important factors in college admissions.

Chapter 13

College Visits and Information Sessions

I t's never too early to start looking at colleges, and there's no better way to learn more about a college than to visit it yourself.

Students in secondary school, who have the financial resources, should start visiting colleges of interest as soon as possible.

COLLEGE CAMPUS VISITS

Visiting the college is an important part of your college decision process. Visiting a school gives you a chance to ask questions, take a tour, sit in on classes, and obtain an overall feeling of the college's atmosphere. Going around to the different colleges will give you a chance to compare them and gain a better idea of which college is right for you.

On a campus visit, you'll see much, much more than you can see in a brochure or online. College marketing doesn't typically show the campus when it's buried under ten feet of snow.

How should I prepare for the visit?
Do a little research on the college before you visit. Start by looking through the brochures and on the college's website. On the tour, you can then ask questions about the things you're interested in knowing more about.

Make sure you visit the school's website to schedule a campus tour and information session at least two weeks before you plan to go. If you are in your final year of school, consider scheduling an interview. But make sure you are very familiar with the college and have done some interview preparation before deciding to do so. (See chapter 6 for interview preparation.)

When is the best time to visit a campus?

You will get the best school experience when school is in session during the regular academic year. You can meet students and get a feel for the rhythm of the campus. You may even get a chance to sit in on a class. If you visit the school while it is not in session, you may find yourself touring a deserted campus.

Call the college or check out a school's academic calendar to find out when breaks, holidays, and exam periods are scheduled. You don't want to show up when no one is around or tours are not being given.

Mondays through Thursdays are the best days for visits. On Fridays, faculty and students are focusing more on the weekend ahead.

High schools and colleges are on different schedules, so there may be good opportunities for you to visit on holidays that fall on weekdays and during spring break. Many colleges begin their fall semester in mid-August, so also consider visiting in late summer and early September, before your high school semester begins.

You can also visit schools after you've been accepted. Many colleges invite accepted candidates to spend time on campus to encourage them to enroll. However, waiting this long will not give you much time for visits.

What should I bring along?

Wear comfortable walking shoes since the tour should include a walk around the campus. You will also want to bring a pen and a notebook to write down any notes that will help you remember the school. If you have a smartphone, in the notes section, you can create notes for each school. You can also use your phone to take photos and videos. Make sure it's fully charged. If you don't have a smartphone, pack a camera or video camera. Pictures will help you remember more details.

117

Whom should I talk to?

Talk with as many people as you can. This list can include professors, admissions officers, students, and the international student office. International students should try to talk to students from their country. Ask them about their experience at the school.

Admissions officers can give you answers about application deadlines, timing, and what the school is generally looking for in a student. Professors can give you a feel of what they expect—but because all professors are different, try to talk to as many as you can. Some schools even offer the opportunity to sit in on some of their classes. Look to students to give you the real information about the college as a whole. Since students are not employed by the college, they will usually give you the most honest answers.

If you can, talk to a student in your intended major. Find out how the program runs and what opportunities are available. If you do not know what you want to major in, talk to a few students in different majors and get to know the options. Talking to a professor in your major can also give you more insight on a particular program. Meetings with students and professors can be arranged through the admissions office or by contacting the department of interest.

What questions should I ask?

You should ask all the questions you need to get the information you want. These can range from which professors are recommended and the best classes to take, to study-abroad opportunities. We do recommend, however, staying away from asking the tour guide questions about the school that you can find on the website or in the catalog. We also don't recommend that you ask the admissions representatives all about the social life. Save that for any students you meet. We've provided some questions on the next page that you can use as a starting point.

No matter whom you talk to, be positive, polite, and intellectually curious. Ask questions and make sure you take notes!

118

INTERNATIONAL COLLEGE COUNSELORS TIP:
If you plan to have an admission interview, or if you want to meet with a particular professor or financial aid officer, make an appointment. Call or email the school to arrange this before you make the trip.

Other College Visit Options to Consider

Stay overnight.
Students interested in a school can stay overnight on a number of college campuses. An overnight visit can give you a real feel of the campus and a deeper understanding of the college. For one, you get to stay in a dorm. You can also get to meet students who go to the school, as well as other people who are also applying to the school. If a school does not have official opportunities to stay overnight, consider contacting a student that you know and see if you can stay with him or her for a night or weekend. A longer visit will give you more information about the school, the students, and the community. The more you know, the easier it is to determine whether a school is the right fit for you.

Shadow a student.
Ask the college if you can "shadow" a student. This means you can spend a day with a student, attending classes with him or her, and engaging in social events. This is a great way to learn what a day in the life of a student at a particular college is like. Many colleges offer this option. Check the college website for information on this opportunity or contact the admissions office.

Any last thoughts?
Yes. Be sure to "sign in" with legible handwriting. This will let the school know you were there and demonstrated interest by visiting. This will also give you a good conversation topic for any admissions interviews. If you visit a school, make sure you mention it at some time during the interview (assuming your interview is off-campus).

Consider stopping into the International Admissions Office. These are the individuals who will be reading your application, and it can't hurt to stop in and ask a thoughtful question or two. If you are concerned about finances, don't hesitate to stop in the Office of Financial Aid. They can answer any of your questions quickly and effectively.

Don't miss the opportunity to check out the local community. You will want to know whether the size of the town is right for you and if there's ample entertainment available, among other things.

Also, when you're back at home after your visit, send thank-you notes or a thank-you email within forty-eight hours. Make sure to remember your guide's name, any interviewers you met with, and the professors you talked to. This will renew your name in their minds, and this can make a difference.

College Visit Follow-Up

Dear Mr./Ms. [LAST NAME OF PERSON WITH WHOM YOU MET],

I visited [NAME OF COLLEGE] on [date of visit]. [If you asked questions] I wanted to thank you for taking the time to talk to me and answer my questions.

[If you did not get a chance to ask a question] It was a pleasure meeting you. I had one quick follow-up question that I hoped you'd be able to answer. [Insert question here].

After visiting the school, exploring the campus, and meeting with you, my dream of attending [NAME OF COLLEGE] has been solidified. Thank you again for your help. I look forward to applying to [NAME OF COLLEGE].
Sincerely,

[Your name and high school]
[Home country]

COLLEGE TOUR, INFORMATION SESSION, AND INFORMATIONAL MEETING SAMPLE QUESTIONS

Academic Questions

▸ Are professors accessible outside of class?

▸ What is the typical way to get in touch with a professor? Email? Phone call?

▸ Do you usually get in all the classes that you need to register for?

▸ How many courses are taught by professors, and how many by a teaching assistant?

▸ What are the most popular majors? The least popular majors?

▸ What is the grading system like?

▸ What is the study-abroad program here like?

Financial Questions

▸ If you have financial need, does the school offer financial aid packages to international students? Can the packages meet all of your demonstrated need?

▸ Are there work-study jobs available on campus? Off campus?

▸ If you don't qualify for work-study, what jobs are available near campus that you could apply for?

Safety Questions

▸ How safe is the campus? How often are crimes reported?

▸ Is the campus well lit?

▸ How large is the campus security force? Does it patrol the campus regularly?

▸ Is there a pickup or shuttle service for students walking at night? How late does it run?

- What services are offered by the campus health center? How large is it?

Campus Questions

- Does the campus seem too big? Too small?

- Does the campus look well cared for?

- Do you feel comfortable and safe?

- Do most of the students seem to be like you, or are they completely different?

- If you are required to live on campus your first year, are you OK with this?

- Are the dorms single sex or coed?

- Do freshmen live in their own dorms?

- Are the dorms quiet or noisy? Do they seem crowded? Can you see yourself living there?

- What are the rules for students living in dorms?

- Can students remain in dorms over academic breaks?

- What types of meal plans are available?

- What hours are food services available?

Social Questions

- What do students do on weekends? Stay on campus? Go home?

- What are the most popular extracurricular activities?

- What are the biggest student hangouts in and around campus?

- Are there sororities and fraternities on campus? What percentage of students participate?

- Are parties allowed on campus?

Athletic Questions

▸ Is the college considered an athletic school?

▸ What sports are the most popular?

▸ Do athletes have to miss a lot of classes in order to participate in games?

▸ Do athletes have their own dorms?

▸ What's the condition of the playing fields and the sports equipment?

Questions for Students

▸ Why did you choose this particular college?

▸ What's your least favorite thing about the school?

▸ Are the professors helpful and accessible?

▸ What do you do on a typical weekend?

▸ If you had to do it over again, would you still choose to attend?

Community Questions

▸ Do you like the surrounding city or town?

▸ Is the city or town big enough for your taste? Does it have enough entertainment for you?

▸ What is the international community like?

▸ How easy is it to get to places off campus? Will you need a car? Are there places within walking distance?

▸ What is the city's public transportation system like?

International Student Office Questions

▸ What is the international population of this college?

▸ What is the percentage of international students on campus?

▸ How does the school support international students?

- ▸ From which countries do students come?

- ▸ Does the university offer any scholarships for international students?

- ▸ Are there any specific requirements for students from my country?

- ▸ What type of visa or documentation do I need?

- ▸ What are the housing options for international students?

- ▸ What housing or resources are available during holidays and breaks?

- ▸ Are there any student representatives from my country to whom I can speak?

ATTENDING INFORMATION SESSIONS

Attending information sessions can help you learn about colleges and, as importantly, will enable colleges to learn about your interest in their school.

College Campus Information Sessions
At a campus information session, representatives from a university will present information about their institution and answer questions about the admissions process. Students, and parents who accompany their students, will learn what distinguishes one school from another, what colleges look for in the selection process, and what one can do to enhance the college application. You will also gain insights into campus life, financial aid, and the scholarship process. There is always a question-and-answer period at the end. Generally, each session lasts approximately an hour. Current students and/or alumni may also present, depending on where and when the information session is held. Sometimes food is served, and sometimes it is not.

Almost every school offers information sessions on campus. Call a school or check its website to see the schedule.

For Students Unable to Visit Universities

If money, distance, or time is an issue, do not feel as though you must visit a college in order to get in. University representatives travel around the world reaching out to students.

You can also attend an online college fair where you can speak directly with admission representatives and alumni from U.S. colleges.

Find out about upcoming college information sessions or college fairs and get invited to them by going to a school's website and signing up on the admissions page to learn more. Almost every school has a "contact us" page. Also, requesting this information shows a college you are interested in it.

College Representatives' Visits to High Schools

In some cases, college informational meetings can take place at your high school. A college's representative visits the high school, and students may be invited or can ask to attend. Ask to attend the representative visits for the schools that interest you. This is a great way to get to know a college and demonstrate interest to the admissions staff.

Schools let their students know about these visits in different ways. Some post notices near the guidance counselor's office. Others post them on a website. Make sure you know how your school is letting people know which college reps are visiting and when, and check back often.

Be sure to fill out the contact form a representative is likely to hand out.

If a school representative comes to your high school and you don't bother to attend the meeting, an admissions officer might conclude that you are not that interested in the school. This is a big missed opportunity.

After the school representative's visit to your school, send a thank-you note or email within forty-eight hours after the visit. Here is a sample letter, but make sure to personalize it with your information.

Informational Meeting Follow-Up

Dear Mr./Ms. [LAST NAME OF PERSON WITH WHOM YOU MET],

Thank you very much for visiting [NAME OF YOUR HIGH SCHOOL] on [date of visit]. I learned a lot about [NAME OF COLLEGE]. I was particularly impressed when you mentioned [Insert interesting fact here that the representative shared. For example, an additional program in international relations, the diverse population, a specific club or organization, etc.].

I appreciate you coming to talk to us. I look forward to applying to [NAME OF COLLEGE].

Sincerely,
[Your name]

College Fairs
College fairs span the globe and visit almost every major metropolitan area in the world. You will find them to be outstanding opportunities to learn about a wide variety of schools. At a college fair you can attend helpful seminars, meet school representatives, and collect information on:

▸ Admission requirements

▸ Financial aid

▸ College majors and courses

▸ Admission requirements

▸ Life on campus

▸   Scholarships

Generally, each school will have a table or booth stocked with informational brochures. A representative will often be there to answer any questions you may have about the college. Some college fairs are even attended by actual admissions officers—whom you can talk to! You can also pick up a lot of pens, bags, and other giveaway items.

Fairs are designed to help you cross some colleges off your list and discover new ones to add.

The majority of college fairs happen to be free and open to the public. International students and those who are unable to travel to the college fair locations should consider attending virtual college fairs. One of the most popular hosts for this is College Week Live. You can see their offerings at http://www.collegeweeklive.com.

To find more college fairs, use the search engine phrase: "college fair."

INTERNATIONAL COLLEGE COUNSELORS TIP:
After meeting anyone connected to a college of interest, give them your contact information and ask them for a business card. If you meet a college representative virtually, ask them for contact information. It will show that you're interested in the university. It will also give you contact information, which is useful for follow-up questions and thank-you notes.

127

Below is a sample thank-you note/email that is clear, concise, and appreciative.

College Fair Visit Follow-Up

Dear Mr./Ms. [NAME OF PERSON WITH WHOM YOU MET],

I attended the [NAME OF COLLEGE FAIR] on [date of visit]. [If you asked questions] I wanted to thank you for taking the time to talk to me and answer my questions.

[If you did not get a chance to ask a question] It was a pleasure meeting you. I had one quick follow-up question that I hoped you'd be able to answer. [Insert question here.]

Thank you again for your help, and I look forward to applying to [NAME OF COLLEGE].

Sincerely,

[Your name and high school]

Online College Fairs

Virtual college fairs allow you to meet U.S. admission representatives without leaving your home. A number of sites offer these live online chats. Some virtual events include a number of colleges at one time. Other virtual events feature one school.

Online you can attend helpful seminars, meet school representatives, and collect information on:

▸ Admission requirements

▸ Financial aid

- College majors and courses

- Admission requirements

- Life on campus

- Scholarships

Two popular sites for virtual college events are: www.CollegeFairsOnline.com and www.CollegeWeekLive.com. Check their websites for specific event dates.

Sometimes virtual college fairs are held with presentations in Spanish.

VIRTUAL TOURS

A number of schools offer video tours of campus. Others stream live webcams onto their websites, offer photorealistic tours, and have interactive campus maps online.

They're fun and another tool for students to use, but they're not a replacement for actual campus visits.

What virtual tours are especially good for is helping to weed out colleges you're possibly interested in. They're also helpful for international students with difficulty traveling.

For virtual tours, take a look at

- CampusTours: www.campustours.com

- eCampusTours: www.ecampustours.com

Also visit a college's website and see if they offer one there.

Chapter 14

Choosing a College List

Choosing a college list is a really big decision, and up to this point in your life, you've probably never had to make a decision as big as this one.

You're not alone. There are thousands and thousands and thousands of high school students around the world feeling as anxious as you are.

What is vital for your success is to make the process as stress-free as possible.

Knowledge is power, and the more you know about different colleges, the easier it will be to find the right college fit for you. What's good for one student isn't necessarily the best for another. You're not "competing" against anyone but yourself.

Dream big, but be open to compromise. You may be pleasantly surprised.

At International College Counselors, we are very concerned about "fit." I remember talking to a student who transferred from Duke because he simply did not like to watch basketball. And, while he appreciated his school's academics and spirit, so much of the social life revolved around basketball that he often felt like an outsider. Clearly, the fit of this school was not for him.

STEP ONE: DO A PRELIMINARY COLLEGE SEARCH

Hop on the Internet.
Familiarize yourself with what's out there. Get on your computer and start looking at college websites. Is there a college you've heard of that sounded interesting? Take a look at the website. Type the word "college" into a search engine and pick a city. See what comes up. Type

in "college" with different words, like "best weather," "happiest," "friendliest," or "career opportunities." If something looks interesting, take a deeper look. Did a friend, parent, teacher, or coach mention a college to you in passing? Look it up.

Enhance your search by visiting college search websites.
Princeton Review: www.princetonreview.com
Kaplan: www.kaplan.com
College Board: www.collegeboard.com

Take a look at websites for college rankings.
Website URLs are listed later in this chapter, but make sure to read my thoughts on college rankings.

Check out college guides.
These may be available at your high school or local library. You can also find them at bookstores and online at Amazon.com.

Take advantage of the college visits at your high school.
See chapter 13 for more information on college visits.

Attend college information sessions.
See chapter 13 for more about college information sessions.

Attend college fairs online or nearby.
See chapter 13 for more information on college fairs.

Ask around.
Talk to people you respect. Find out where they went to college and what it meant to them. Do you have a dream job? Ask human resources directors where they recruit.

STEP TWO: MAKE A LIST OF WHAT YOUR COLLEGE MUST HAVE

Write down the top five things your college must have. These are the deal-breakers. If a college doesn't have these five things, you're going to cross it off your list. I would highly recommend that one of these deal-breakers be your choice of major. If robotics is a career you're interested in, it's going to be very hard to explore the possibilities if the school has no resources for you to work with.

Make another list of the five things "I wish the college has." This list will help you weed down your list, but don't use it to cross schools off the list completely—yet. If an extracurricular you really want is not offered at a school, don't cross the college off the list. Open the door for opportunity. This may be a chance for you to start an organization at your college. College is the ideal time to explore leadership opportunities.

International students may benefit from a large foreign community when trying to acclimate to American life. While doing research on colleges, international students should take a look at the percentage of international students who attended the school in the previous academic year. Students can even look into how many students come from a particular country.

Make sure you also check a map. The United States is very big. Many U.S. states are as big as some countries. If you want to be near New York City, New York, you do not want to be in Buffalo, New York. Also, you may want to consider how long it takes to get to a college. Will you need to take one flight? Three flights and a bus? How about time zones? There is a three-hour time difference between the East Coast and West Coast of the United States. These travel and communication decisions can make a difference for some students.

STEP THREE: DO IN-DEPTH RESEARCH

Go online again.
If you're interested in a college, scour its official website. All colleges have one. Think of yourself as a detective, and look beyond the obvious facts like campus size, location, courses of study, and degree programs. Investigate campus activities, study-abroad programs, student organizations, special programs, etc. Also follow them on Twitter, Facebook, Google+, Flickr, or whatever your social networking preference.

Think about what you want.
College experiences differ greatly. A name brand isn't necessarily going to make a school the right fit for you. A better place to start is by considering academics, campus life, location, student profile, and financial aid. You will need to do some research to answer some of the following questions. Answers can be found online or by calling/emailing the school. Then it's up to you to decide how you feel about what you learn.

SAMPLE QUESTIONS TO ASK DURING YOUR RESEARCH

Academic Questions
► Is there a program in my field? How strong is it?

► What classes are offered?

► Who is teaching in my area of study?

► How many students are in each class?

► What have graduates of the program gone on to do?

► What kind of real-life opportunities might be available to me as a student in this program (hands-on activities, internships, volunteer work, opportunities to meet potential employers)?

► Can I study abroad?

Campus Life Questions

- What kinds of activities are available?

- What are the sports options?

- What's the atmosphere like on campus?

- How important are fraternities and sororities?

- How safe is the campus?

- What kinds of student services are offered?

- What resources are available to help students succeed?

- Do I feel like I will fit in?

- Are there other students from my country at the college?

- Does the school meet my special needs? (For more information on special needs, see chapter 15.)

School Size and Location Questions

- How many students are at the school?

- Is it a city campus, a rural campus, or a college-town campus?

- What is the typical weather?

- How far is it from home? Is there a direct flight?

- What is the cost to travel home on holidays and weekends? How much time will the trip take?

School Profile Questions

- Does the college have a diverse student population?

- What is the SAT/ACT range?

- Are my scores above or below these numbers?

- What is the average GPA?

- Is my GPA comparable?

- What is the minimum TOEFL or IELTS score required?

Financial Aid Questions
- What kind of financial aid is available for international students?

- How will the amount of financial aid I receive be determined?

- What grants and scholarships are available, not just loans? How do I apply? When are the deadlines?

- What is the tuition rate?

- What might other costs be of attending? (Housing, books, meal plans, etc.)

- Does the college require a certification or statement of finances during the application process or once the student has been accepted?

- Are there resources available to help with these costs?

- What work opportunities are available, on or off campus?

- Can I work and attend classes?

Initially, do not cross off any colleges because of cost. Many colleges and countries offer financial aid, scholarships, and other help that make them far more affordable than they first appear. I discuss financial aid in depth in chapter 19.

STEP FOUR: GET A SECOND/THIRD/FOURTH/ETC. OPINION

Talk to alumni.
On most college websites, you can find information on the alumni association. If there are email addresses of an alumni club listed, send an email asking if there would be a representative open to speaking with you or answering a few questions. Do not assume that anyone will be able to talk immediately. It is important to ask politely and set up a time to talk.

135

Be creative. Search the Internet for college-specific phrases in quotes, like, "I graduated from Muhlenberg," or "Since graduating from Princeton…" See what former and current students have to say.

Check out ranking sites where the rankings are based on student reviews:

▸ Students Review: http://www.studentsreview.com

▸ Unigo: http://www.unigo.com/colleges

▸ Niche: http://www.niche.com/colleges

▸ Rate my Professors: http://www.ratemyprofessors.com

Talk to your college counselor.
He or she could give you additional advice and guidance as it applies to your school.

Talk with family, friends, teachers, and mentors.
These are trusted adults whom know you well.

Do a reality check.
Compare your academic profile to the profile of the most recently enrolled class for the colleges you are looking into. Some college websites have this information. Contact the school if you can't find it. This will give you a realistic understanding of what your chances are for getting into a certain school.

After comparing your test scores and grades, look at your list again. If your grades and scores are lower than the middle-range scores of more than four schools on your list, you need to add more schools to your list.

My recommendation is to investigate at least three or four colleges that are not familiar to you. Basic requirements: Each one must offer the field of study that interests you, be appropriately selective for a student with your grades and scores, have a price or financial aid possibilities that you can afford, and have a location where you could happily live.

A new school you learn about just may be your dream school.

STEP FIVE: VISIT SCHOOLS

If you can, visit at least three schools before your final year of secondary school. The Internet is no substitute for an actual college visit. If you can, sit in on a class. See more on college visits in chapter 13.

STEP SIX: CREATE A COLLEGE LIST

Begin your last year of secondary school with a list of eight to ten colleges that interest you.

Do not believe you will only be happy at one school in the world. Oftentimes students "compromise" and go to schools that are not their first choice. Many of these students end up absolutely loving that school, staying there, and feeling quite lucky they didn't go anywhere else. Other students attend another school for one or two years and then transfer. For more on transferring, see chapter 18.

Safety and Reach Schools

Every student's final college lists should have one or two "safety schools" on it. A safety school is a college to which you are almost certain you will be admitted. As importantly, there shouldn't be any schools on your list that you would not be happy to attend.

Reach for your dreams and apply to a few "reach schools." A reach school is one where you are a little below the average range for accepted freshmen. For example, if the average SAT score is 1500 and you have a 1420, you have a low chance of getting accepted, and this is considered a reach. Additionally, the Ivy League colleges and schools like Stanford and MIT are reach schools for just about everyone, as their acceptance rates are so low. If you're in the competitive zone or you play the bassoon and the school is looking for a bassoon player, for example, you just may get in to the school.

U.S. News & World Report College Rankings and Their Meaning

College rankings lists are often considered a "must-read" for most students and their families.

Some of the more well-known rankings lists come from:

- ▸ *U.S. News & World Report*:
     http://colleges.usnews.rankingsandreviews.com/college

- ▸ *Bloomberg Businessweek* (business schools only)
     http://www.bloomberg.com

- ▸ The Princeton Review:
     http://www.princetonreview.com/college/college-rankings.aspx

- ▸ Kiplinger: http://www.kiplinger.com/tools/colleges

- ▸ *Forbes*: http://www.forbes.com/top-colleges/list

- ▸ Niche: https://colleges.niche.com/rankings/

Each organization and publication bases its ranking on multiple statistical measures. Each of these measures may be unique to each ranking. When looking at rankings, look at the measures to see what determined the ranking position.

Parents and students have been using these lists as a way to sort out schools.

Of course, as soon as rankings come out, colleges see them, too. And the administrations of these colleges begin strategizing about how they might move their college up in the ranks. Unsurprisingly, several colleges have been caught climbing the rankings by reinterpreting the meanings of rules, manipulating data, or just flat-out lying.

In my opinion, college rankings are nothing more than relying on the Miss Universe pageant to measure beauty. The only way to truly rank colleges is to consider what the value is to you. Rankings are useful if you consider and weigh the information they give you separate from their final results.

Working with Your Parents
Communication is key for families going through the admissions process. Make sure you have a talk with your parents or guardians as you choose your colleges. Ask their opinion on your choice of colleges, major, location, and, importantly, cost. Be open to listening to them. Be prepared to answer any questions they may have, as well. If you've chosen Celtic language as a possible major, explain to your parents why you chose it and what you plan to do with the degree. If you want to go to college in New York and they ask you why, good answers don't include the phrases "shopping" or "going to clubs." Another good move is to let your parents know that you plan to apply for scholarships and do what you can to help out with this significant financial investment.

If your parents insist you apply to a certain college, do it; don't fight it. It won't hurt and you don't have to commit to a college until the deadline.

Your parents will feel most comfortable if you schedule time at least once every two weeks to update them with what you're doing. Let them know about your test prep, school research, school counselor meetings, and scholarship applications. The more mature you show them you are, the more trust you earn.

Chapter 15

Schools and Programs for Students with Learning Differences

There are support services available for students with learning differences. These services vary in quality and extent from school to school.

As more and more high school students with learning differences are applying to colleges, the schools are prepared to answer questions and provide guidance.

HOW TO CHOOSE A SCHOOL: AN OVERVIEW

Students with learning differences should follow the same steps for choosing and applying to a school as any other student. The more information you have, the more "educated" your decision can be. If you're a student with a learning difference, you need to evaluate schools based on their ability to accommodate your needs.

Good starting resources for students with learning differences who are applying to college include the Learning Disabilities Association of America (http://ldanatl.org) and the *K&W Guide to Colleges for Students with Learning Disabilities* by Marybeth Kravets. This 800-plus-page book profiles over three hundred schools and includes information on services at each college, admissions requirements, and contact information for program administrators.

Start by reviewing your needs.
Sit down with knowledgeable adults—whether they are your parents, your doctor, your therapist, or your college admissions counselor—and start by reviewing your needs. The goal is to better understand your difference and its effect on your college choices. Ask these questions:

- How does my difference affect how I learn?

- What are my academic strengths?

- How do I learn best?

- What strategies do I need to help me learn?

- What facilities may I need?

- What environmental conditions do I need? (For example, if you are in a wheelchair, the best college for you may not be on a rural campus where it snows a lot.)

- What careers am I interested in? (Stay realistic about how any learning or physical needs may influence these career areas.)

Once you have these questions answered, begin building a college list. Once you narrow your college choices, contact the disability services office of each school to determine whether a college has the services and accommodations that can support your needs and meet your specific requirements. Programs, policies, procedures, and facilities must meet the needs of your individual situation.

INVESTIGATE THE SCHOOLS

Most colleges have an office that provides services to students with learning differences, or a person who coordinates these services. This resource can usually be found at a school's counseling center or as part of student services. This office may be referred to by a number of names including the Office of Student Disability Services, Disability Support, Office of Disabled Student Services, and Learning Support Services.

Depending on your difference, here are some questions to ask the disability services representative:

- What documentation must I bring to identify myself as a student with a disability entitled to reasonable accommodation? How

141

current must it be?

- How is confidential information handled?

- Who decides whether I qualify for accommodations?

- Are the accommodations I need available?

- How much advance notice is needed to have textbooks recorded on tape?

- Is tutoring provided? What is the cost?

- Are waivers or substitutions granted to students who, because of their differences, cannot pass certain courses, such as foreign languages or statistics?

- Are basic skills, study skills, time management, or organizing classes offered? Are they available for credit? Can they be counted as hours toward full-time status? What is the cost?

- Is there a support group on campus for students with disabilities?

- Is there adaptive technology available?

- How many students does the support program serve?

- How many disability specialists work with the program full-time and part-time?

- Are disability specialists available for ongoing counseling, guidance, and support?

- Does the school offer specialized academic advising for students with differences?

- Does disability support help to communicate each student's needs to the appropriate professors?

- Is there a physician at student health who has experience treating and prescribing medication for my condition?

- Does the office have a listing of professionals in the area who are experienced in treating my condition?

I also recommend you visit each school's website for college disability services to get an idea of eligibility requirements, resources, services and accommodations, documentation required, available academic support, and policies.

You may also want to ask to meet with one or two other students with learning differences enrolled in the school who currently receive support services. They are often the best resource for practical information about the strengths and weaknesses of the program.

HOW TO MAKE YOURSELF A STRONG CANDIDATE FOR ADMISSIONS

Succeed to the best of your abilities! It is important to know that a school cannot deny your admission because of a disability if you meet the basic requirements for admission. These basic requirements include meeting application deadlines, grades, and college entrance exam scores. In fact, you don't even need to tell a school you have a disability on your application, unless you want an academic adjustment.

What you must do is keep your grades up and become involved in extracurricular activities—just like any other student. Disabled or not, students must meet school standards for admission.

INTERNATIONAL COLLEGE COUNSELORS NOTE:
The Americans with Disabilities Act (ADA) requires educational institutions at all levels, public and private, to provide equal access to their programs, services, and facilities to students, employees, and members of the public, regardless of disability.

TO TELL OR NOT TO TELL

Whether you should tell a college about your disability early in the admissions process is up to you.

Telling a college about a disability early in the admissions process is often recommended for applicants who need to provide explanation. For example, a disabled student may need to explain why a standardized test score appears low when compared with outstanding grades. However, applicants with strong grades and test scores should think twice before disclosing any learning issues, especially if there is no reason to.

While it is unethical for a school to discriminate based on disability, this does not mean it cannot happen. Whatever your decision, consider that you may prefer to attend a school that is going to be sensitive to your difference and help you be successful.

THE APPLICATION

If you decide to tell the college about your learning difference, we recommend that you describe your difference in a letter to the appropriate school personnel and keep a copy of the letter.

You can also call attention to your difference in your main essay. However, if you choose to do this, the essay must be positive and show how you can still succeed. For example, a good essay would say how you were diagnosed with dyslexia in a lower grade and are now in a top math class. You may not be getting a top grade, but the explanation puts the accomplishment in perspective.

We discuss this more in chapter 4, but do not try to write an essay that tries to make an admissions officer feel sorry for you. This doesn't work.

Also, be prepared to send copies of your psycho-educational evaluation, testing records, and any other assessments of your abilities directly to the school. If the documentation for the disability or difference is in another language, it must be translated into English. Only documentation in English is accepted.

TESTING ADJUSTMENTS FOR STUDENTS WITH LEARNING DIFFERENCES

Students with physical disabilities or learning differences can receive special accommodations on standardized tests, including the following:

- SAT
- SAT Subject Tests
- ACT
- PSAT
- TOEFL / IELTS
- Advanced Placement Program (AP) exams
- ASSET
- COMPASS

ACT/SAT/PSAT/AP Exams

As a student with a learning difference, you must request special accommodations through the testing companies. Most students work with their schools to have the school submit accommodation requests online. If your school does not have someone to help you, the testing companies require a separate from to be filled out. You will be asked to provide documentation of your learning difference. For details, visit the ACT website (http://www.act.org) and the College Board website (http://www.collegeboard.com).

TOEFL and IELTS

To request accommodations for a learning difference or health-related need, you must register by mail. Do this well in advance of the date you plan to take the test. The test administrators must review and respond to your accommodations request before the test can be scheduled. Details, directions on how to request accommodations, and contact information is available on the TOEFL or IELTS websites (https://www.ets.org/toefl) or (https://www.ielts.org).

Testing accommodations may include:

▸ Extended testing time and additional rest breaks

▸ A sign language interpreter

▸ An audiocassette or large-screen version of the testScreen magnification

▸ Transcripts of audio elements in the speaking and writing sections

▸ Braille editions

▸ A scribe to write answers on a test-taker's behalf

ASSET and COMPASS

Test-taking accommodations also apply to the ASSET (Assessment of Skills for Successful Entry and Transfer) and COMPASS (Computer Adaptive Placement Assessment and Support System) tests. These are short placement exams often required by community colleges. These exams are designed to help identify your strengths and needs. More information on these exams can be found at http://www.act.org/compass and http://www.act.org/asset/index.html.

Testing accommodations may include:

▸ Individual administration of the test

▸ Audiocassette tape or large-print test editions

▸ Special answer sheets

▸ Extended testing time and additional rest breaks

▸ An interpreter

▸ Braille editions

NOTE: Remember, if the documentation for your disability or learning difference is in another language, it must be translated into English. The schools will only accept documentation in English.

INTERNATIONAL COLLEGE COUNSELORS TIP:
If you are given extra time on the SAT and ACT, this information is kept confidential by the testing companies. We recommend that you apply for accommodations in your first or second year of high school. It takes time to apply, gives you time to appeal, and you do not want to take the test if you fear you will not do well without the accommodation.

Do not take the SAT or ACT if you believe you are eligible for accommodations before getting those accommodations. If you take the test without accommodations and do "well," the SAT and ACT companies will use that as "proof" that you don't need the accommodation. But what you think is "good" may be different from what the College Board considers "good."

We once worked with a student named Byron who had straight As and also a learning difference. He wanted to attend Harvard or another Ivy League school. Before Byron started working with us, he took the SAT before applying for extra time. The College Board thought his score was "good." We knew he could have done better with extra time. Unfortunately, Byron was unable to get his extra time for a retake of the test. Thankfully, since the College Board and ACT are two separate companies, he was able to get the extra time for the ACT. He did far better on that exam.

FINANCIAL AID

Disability-related expenses may be factored into the cost of attendance. When you apply for financial aid, inform the financial aid office of any disability-related expenses.

Possible disability-related expenses include:

▸ Services for personal care attendants

▸ Special education equipment related to your disability and its maintenance

▸ Special transportation

▸ Medical expenses relating directly to your disability not covered by insurance

If the financial aid process becomes overwhelming, ask for help. A college's office of disability service and housing services will answer your questions and help you complete this process.

Some private foundations help students, including international students, with disability-related expenses.

ONCE YOU'RE ACCEPTED TO COLLEGE

Don't overlook the details. You will need to take certain steps to ensure everything runs smoothly. Students receive services related to a disability only if they:

▸ Contact the coordinator of disability services.

▸ Provide the required documentation. (Make sure your tests are updated.)

▸ Request services each term or semester.

Colleges do not have to identify you as a person with a disability. To get your accommodations, you need to find the college's disability services center and go through their eligibility process. Call the school's office that provides services to students with disabilities for information and help. Remember, reasonable accommodations are intended to "level the playing field" between disabled and non-disabled students. This means the accommodations are designed to help a student with disabilities participate in a program. It does not mean a program will be greatly changed in course content or course standards.

Common accommodations include extended time for test-taking, assistive technology, oral reports instead of written reports, and alternate forms of class projects. In college, determining what is reasonable is mostly decided by your professors and disability resource professionals.

Colleges are not allowed to charge students with disabilities more than it charges students who do not have disabilities for any programs or activities.

Limitations to Consider
Colleges are not required to do any of the following:

▸   Make any accommodations that would lower or change their academic standards to accommodate a disability.

▸   Make any changes in programs or activities that would fundamentally change the nature of the program.

▸   Provide accommodations that would cause an undue financial burden. This includes personal attendants, readers for personal use or study, or other personal services such as tutoring and typing services.

Chapter 16

Community College, Alternative Schools, the Gap Year, and Alternative Opportunities

You don't have to go to a four-year college right away. Some students benefit from a year off to work, study, or travel, and these experiences allow them to be better, more engaged students. Some students choose to apply to college, gain admission, and then defer their entrance, while others wait to apply until after they have had an alternative experience.

You don't have to achieve a four-year college degree to find a career that fits your personality, interests, and talents. You don't need a four-year college degree to build a successful career. While you may want to eventually consider getting a four-year college degree, choosing an alternative course of action is something worth considering. For some people, the flexibility of these alternatives allows them to explore their choices of careers and locations. Whatever you choose to do, the important thing is that you choose something that keeps your life and career moving in a forward direction.

COMMUNITY COLLEGE

Community colleges, also known as two-year colleges or junior colleges, are one of the largest and fastest-growing sectors of higher education. Community colleges usually offer two-year programs that provide an "associates degree." Attendance at a community college can serve as a path leading to a four-year school (including an Ivy League institution) or straight into a career. Starting at a community college also offers a number of other advantages, including the following:

Easier Admissions Requirements
All students are accepted to community college, regardless of past academic performance, if they've graduated from high school or have

150

a high school equivalency diploma. The SAT and ACT are not required for entrance into many community colleges. Many community colleges do not require TOEFL or IELTS scores for admissions, either.

Cost Savings
Tuition and fees are typically much lower at community colleges than at four-year colleges, even the public ones. Students can save thousands of dollars by first attending a community college.

Opportunities to Explore
Community colleges offer students the chance to explore their interests before committing to a major. This can save you a lot of money if you are undecided.

Certificates and/or Diplomas
The two-year programs at a community college can earn you an associate or liberal arts degree. Their curriculum can also include specialized career training and certification. Some schools even offer four-year degrees.

Career Guidance
Many community colleges offer extensive support to ensure a student's success, including career guidance, assessments, and a career road map.

Transfer Credits
Four-year schools accept community college students as transfer students. Most also accept some or all credits earned at a community college, though each school has different policies regarding such acceptance of credits. See chapter 18 on transferring these credits. Some four-year colleges partner with two-year colleges to smooth out the transfer process, even allowing students to enter the four-year institution as college juniors.

Basic Requirement Completion
You will need to get your general, basic graduation requirements out of

the way one way or another. Community colleges are good places to earn these credits.

Transcript Improvement

Taking classes at a community college can help you to increase your grade point average (GPA), so if you didn't meet the minimum admissions requirements at the four-year colleges with your high school grades, you can have a second chance. Attending a community college also shows the four-year institutions that you are serious about your education.

Scholarships and Grants

Good grades in a community college can help you earn scholarships and grants later on, a number of which are specifically allotted for students who attended community college.

ALTERNATIVE SCHOOLS—VISUAL OR PERFORMING ARTS SCHOOLS

When it comes to applying to colleges as a prospective visual or performing arts major, you must approach the admissions process with a great deal of passion for your career. Admission requirements usually include auditions or portfolios, which can be both time-consuming and nerve-racking.

Most important, students need to find the right school for their talents. Here are some tips to follow when applying to visual or performing arts schools:

Look beyond the elite schools.

Schools such as New York University, Juilliard, the Rhode Island School of Design, the University of Southern California, the University of Michigan, Berklee College of Music, and Carnegie Mellon University are the elitist of the elite for certain visual or performing arts. They are the Harvards and Princetons for the art community. In other words, many students want to attend these schools, but only a few will be accepted. In any given major—from musical theater to music itself—there are other good schools out there. *U.S. News & World Report* offers a listing of such specialty schools. Look into the schools on this list titled "Unranked Specialty Schools: Arts."

Get an honest opinion of your talents.
Before spending the time and money on applying to college for a visual or performing arts degree, get an expert or two to critique your talent. It may be better for your future to pursue your passion as a minor or a club activity.

Know what you need for the audition or portfolio.
Know what the school requires for the admissions process. For example, Cooper Union School of Art sends an at-home test for you to take when you apply. When you attend an audition, make sure you wear appropriate clothes and perform appropriate material.

Attend joint auditions.
Some colleges hold joint auditions—primarily in the United States—that can help students save money. Joint auditions mean a number of schools, colleges that offer a bachelor's degree program in a particular major, get together and hold auditions or review artwork and offer feedback for performers or those who enter their samples. Theater majors, look into the National Unified Auditions. Visual art and design majors, look into National Portfolio Day.

Pay attention to financial aid.
Many art schools and conservatories are expensive. They also tend to offer less financial aid than traditional colleges, which offer a wider range of majors. You can still successfully develop your passion at a traditional school, so don't ignore considering them if you need the financial aid.

GAP YEAR

It's not unusual for students to take some time off before committing to a two- or four-year college. This break is often called a "gap year." The term "gap year" does not have to mean a full calendar year. Some students take off just one semester or a shorter period of time. Reasons for taking a gap year typically include: avoiding burnout, learning a new language, doing volunteer work, cultivating a passion, satisfying curiosity, or attending to a health or family matter.

INTERNATIONAL COLLEGE COUNSELORS TIP:
Even if you plan to take a gap year off, apply to colleges during your last year of secondary school. Getting application materials together and meeting deadlines during this time is much easier than waiting to do this in the middle of your gap year. If you are accepted to a school and decide to defer admission, look on the school's website for its policies and requirements in this regard. Some schools require your reasons for deferment to be submitted in writing to the dean of admission, along with a deposit. Make sure you meet all of the deadlines to reserve your place in the next year's freshman class, and that you have an understanding of the school's policies. Not all colleges will allow deferred admissions, and some won't give college credit for any work you do during the deferral period.

Note: Even if a college allows for a deferment period, many schools won't allow deferrals for less than a year. Also, if the school does allow you to start midyear, on-campus housing or financial aid may not be available. Check with the housing office and find out what impact, if any, taking a year off will have on your college experience. If you have been offered financial assistance, it may not be guaranteed the next year. Plus, any money you earn during your year off may affect your financial aid eligibility, so be sure to check with the financial aid office. Also check with the admissions office to see if your application will need to be updated after the deferment period is over.

Gap year options range from different activities to different lengths of time. Some of the more common gap year options include:

Securing an internship
An internship is a paid or unpaid position that gives you the opportunity to explore your interests and/or get some training for your future career. If you're thinking about securing an internship before

attending college, look for employers where you can explore a specific interest. See chapter 10 for more information on internships.

Traveling

Visiting new places, both in the United States and abroad, is a great way to acquire valuable life experience and gain perspective on what you want to do with your life. There are many ways to explore the world, some of which don't require a lot of money. Options include student exchange programs, teaching a foreign language abroad, volunteering in the United States or with an international charitable group, becoming a nanny for a family in another country, or even taking a job on a cruise ship. If you do travel, make sure you get to know the local customs and culture. Learning a foreign language can give you a huge boost up on the career ladder. Staying in the United States is also a good way to strengthen your English skills.

Safety alert: If you look for exchange or employment opportunities abroad, make sure you work with a reputable company.

Volunteering

You can gain valuable experience and explore possible career paths through volunteer work during your gap year. There are many opportunities to make a difference in this world. If you're thinking about volunteering, consider options that allow you to explore a specific interest, such as health care, teaching, or environmental conservation. A number of websites can help you find such volunteer opportunities. Type the words "volunteer work find" into a search engine and see what results come up.

Attend a gap year program.

A number of companies have gap year programs designed to help students discover gap year opportunities. A year planned by one of these companies can include work opportunities, study abroad, cultural study programs, language classes, and more. Gap year programs typically cost less than a year of college, but they can still be expensive. To learn what programs are available, type the words "gap year programs" into a search engine.

Start your own business.
Begin your own career path by starting your own business. There are many entrepreneurial business opportunities out there. What you need to do is find your own niche. If you decide to do this, you must do your research and work out a potential business plan. Consider your strengths, interests, and skills as honestly as possible.

ALTERNATIVE EDUCATION OPPORTUNITIES

Apprenticeships
Apprenticeships mean that you learn on the job. If you have an interest in a particular trade, such as computer programming or construction, you have the option to take an apprenticeship or seek out job experience in the trade. Apprenticeships will give you valuable experience through in-depth training and will guide you toward advancement by helping you with the certifications or licenses you need to succeed.

Some professions for which apprenticeships are typical include:

- Construction worker

- Pharmacy assistant (many of these go on to study to become full-fledged pharmacists)

- Plumber

- Carpenter

- Photographer

- Animal breeder

- Baker/chef

- Barber

- Jeweler

▸ Mechanic

Trade School
Specialized trade schools offer classes and specialized training to enter certain careers. Programs can include automobile repair, computer programming, technology, and cosmetology.

Certification and Massive Online Open Courses (MOOCs)
If you are considering a profession like personal trainer, look online to see what options you have for certification. You can also take online courses. This is a good way to explore your interests and continue your education at the same time. There are a number of opportunities to take courses for free. Look into Massive Open Online Courses, also called MOOCs. Schools including MIT, Harvard, Duke, Yale, Stanford, UCLA, Carnegie Mellon, and the University of California, Berkeley offer these classes, many of which are free via the Internet, in subjects ranging from artificial intelligence and chemistry to finance and sociology. A few of the larger organizations offering MOOCs include Coursera, edX, and Udacity.

Paying Job
If you're thinking about getting a job before you go to college, stay away from companies that usually hire teenagers for part-time work; instead apply to employers and companies where you can either start on a definite career path or explore a specific interest. At this time of your life, no job is too small if it relates to your ultimate career goals. Even those who start in the mailroom can work their way up. But be sure to start with employers whose services or products interest you.

Chapter 17

Choosing a Major

Anumber of students say they "always knew" what they wanted to do with their lives. As such, it's easy for them to know what they want to major in. Then there are the majority of students—those with no idea what they really want to do with their lives.

Either way, it's not the end of the world. What's best is that you pick a major for your college application.

Schools prefer that you fill in a college major on the application because they like to see that you have career ambitions. This is especially important if you are applying to a competitive school or program. I always advise students to pick a major on their applications.

Don't panic if you don't have a major in mind. Understand the game. Picking a major for your college application does not mean you're committed to it forever. You are not locked into anything you write on your college admissions form. Most college students change their major at least once in their college careers. Many others change their major several times. Schools also offer double majors, and some even have triple majors. You can choose to minor in a subject, as well,

Keep your eye on the prize. The college admissions goal is to get into the school of your dreams. Once you're in, you'll have more flexibility. Choosing a major and exploring careers are main reasons you go to college in the first place!

INTERNATIONAL COLLEGE COUNSELORS TIP:
Once you get into a school, changing majors may mean giving up a scholarship, so you need to weigh your options and consider the timing when it comes to switching majors. The most important thing is that the school you attend has the major you ultimately choose. You don't want to find out in your senior year that you love architecture but your

school does not have an architecture program. Thinking ahead can save you time and money on transfer applications!

While we understand that many students are unable to know exactly what they want to do when they graduate, it is good to have a general idea. The reason is that you don't want to attend a college that does not have a major of your interest. For example, if you want to become an engineer, it would be great if the college you choose offers an engineering program. Otherwise, you will have to transfer or attend graduate school to get the credits you will need.

We once worked with a student named Shira who was unsure of what she wanted her major to be. She could not decide, and when pressed, she simply stopped talking. What we recommended was that Shira attend a large college that offered lots of majors and course offerings. This way, she could try out many new courses and not be limited by what the school had to offer.

CHOOSING A MAJOR: WHAT YOU NEED TO DO

To make the college journey easier for yourself, you need to narrow down your choices. Your goal is to create a list of a few majors that interest you the most. Then you should explore those few majors in greater depth before making any commitments.

Examine your interests.
*   What are your interests? What are your passions? What types of things excite you? What activities do you make time for and seek out on your own? What do you feel most comfortable doing?

*   Think about your previous classes. Was there one you liked best? Was it math, science, French, or literature?

*   Think about your hobbies. Do you love programming apps, collecting insects, dancing, or designing clothes? Do you like hiking outdoors, meeting new people, or decorating?

▸ What do you like to read about? Do you like astronomy or nature? Fashion or technology?

▸ What extracurricular activities and clubs were especially enjoyable to you in high school?

Examine your abilities.

▸ Be 100 percent honest. What are you good at? What are your strengths? What are your weaknesses? What unique skills or abilities do you have? Are there things that you're better at than most people?

▸ When thinking about your abilities, think about all aspects of your life—from the extracurricular activities in which you participated to the things you learned about yourself from any summer jobs you worked.

▸ In what school courses were you the best? Are you a natural leader? Do you have an above-average ability to stay organized? Are you good with animals, numbers, or seeing patterns in behavior?

▸ Everyone has different preferences and skills. Choosing a major that taps in to those abilities will put you at an advantage. A superhero gifted with flying abilities doesn't say, "I think I will be the spider guy."

Examine what you value in your life and work.
Examples of values include: being around people, attention to detail, helping others, working under pressure, being creative, being part of a group, and many others. You'll most prefer a career that aligns with your personal values.

Explore the careers that interest you.
Imagine doing something you love and getting paid to do it. What would that something be? What kind of work appeals most to you? Did you see something on TV and think that looked like something you could see yourself doing? Does a family friend hold a job you'd like to

have yourself? Are you planning to take over a family business?

If you are passionate about a particular field, consider all aspects of the career path. Health care, for example, involves more than medicine. You could become a medical researcher, a pharmaceutical representative, or a hospital HR manager. A sports career job title isn't only "athlete." You could become a sports trainer, a nutritionist, a sports journalist, or an event planner. Directing and acting aren't the only film-industry careers. Stay seated in the theater after a film and really watch the credits. You'll see a lot of different jobs and titles scroll across the screen.

Do your research.

▸ Talk to students. Locate college students who are studying in the majors in which you are interested.

▸ Review a college's course catalog. This will give you an idea of all the majors from which to choose. It will also give you some insight into what the required courses are and the specialized tracks.

▸ Talk to your academic advisor.

▸ Consult with family and friends. They know you best and can offer some good insight into who you are and what you are good at.

▸ Go online. The Internet contains a vast number of resources concerning various majors and careers.

▸ Connect. Be proactive. See if you can get in touch with someone who is involved with the career or job in which you are interested. Send them a nice note, and maybe you'll get a reply.

▸ Attend club meetings of academically focused clubs, such as Future Doctors or Future Business Leaders.

▸ Attend career-related events, like speaking tours or seminars. Oftentimes you can find these listed on community event calendars.

- Get tested. There are many self-assessment tests, both free and those that require a fee, that can help you determine what you might want to do for your career.

- The Riley Guide, at http://www.rileyguide.com/assess.html, is one such test with links to various other test-assessment websites.

- Attend a career fair.

- Spend some time after school or during winter/spring/summer break shadowing someone who has a career that interests you.

Do a reality check.
Be honest with yourself. If you don't like kids, cross "primary school teacher" off your list. If you're not a competitive person, you aren't going to thrive in investment banking, dance, or public relations. If you don't like science or math, then no matter how promising and lucrative an engineering career sounds, you're going to be miserable. The same goes for being a doctor; you need to be good at science to study medicine. If you're not into detail-oriented work, avoid event planning. If you're not organized in your personal life, it's going to be hard to succeed at human resources. Sometimes there are ways to overcome the obstacles, but it is important to really consider and evaluate whether or not you can—or want—to do so.

Also, begin to look at all the courses you'll need to take in order to graduate with a certain major.

Consider the future.
While everyone wants to do what they love, do not disregard the importance of money or how hard it is to "make it" in certain careers. You may love musical theater, but there are very few people who can make it a full-time career.

If you truly have your heart set on something, it does not mean you should not try to achieve your dream. But you also must move forward knowing the realistic outcome. The same goes for choosing a very, very specific career—studying wild dolphins, for example. It doesn't mean you won't find a job doing so, but it will likely be hard to find the perfect job match. If you go this route, be prepared to compromise somewhere along the way in your career. For example, someone who studies oceanography may consider teaching it one day. Someone who studies drama may find their outlet in community theater while they support themselves in an unrelated field.

Narrow down your choices and then choose a major.
Once you've gone through all these steps, you should have a better idea of the major you are interested in pursuing.

And, as I said before, if you're truly undecided, consider a double major. You can then satisfy an interest with a minor, or go on to grad school.

INTERNATIONAL COLLEGE COUNSELORS TIP:
A few majors have more competitive admission requirements, such as a higher grade point average (GPA), higher test scores, and/or additional coursework. Depending on the college, these majors may require biomedical sciences, business, engineering, or fine arts classes. If you do not have the credentials for the program as specified by the school, consider listing another major on your application.

Chapter 18

Transferring

This is a good chapter for students who want to transfer or are planning to transfer. But even for all students, it's good to know that you have choices. Even after getting into a college, accepting the school's offer, and attending, you can still change your mind if a school is not the right fit for you.

Why do students transfer?

Some reasons students choose to transfer schools include the following:

▸ Their current school does not have a strong program in an area of their interest.

▸ The academics are too challenging or are not challenging enough.

▸ The school is too expensive.

▸ They were rejected from their first-choice school and chose to attend another school with the intention of transferring at a later time to their preferred school.

▸ They graduate from a two-year college and want to move to a four-year one.

▸ They want to enroll in a college with a bigger name or a higher ranking.

▸ They are socially unhappy—for example, a rural campus may prove to be too isolating.

▸ They do not like the weather.

INTERNATIONAL TRANSFER STUDENTS

Transferring from an International School

Colleges have different policies regarding international transfer students. It is best to check each individual school's transfer policy for eligibility and how many credits they will accept.

Some colleges hold the policy that students who transfer must come from a "U.S.-style" college or university. A college or university is considered a U.S.-style institution if:

▸ Courses are offered by term (quarters, semesters, etc.).

▸ A specific grade is given for each course in each term.

▸ The college can provide an English-language transcript showing each course taken and the grades earned in each.

If your school is not a U.S.-style school, some colleges will require that you apply as a first-year student. You will need to check with the individual college's admissions office. Have your current college's course catalogs and syllabi available for an advisor to review when determining transferability of coursework.

For admission purposes, some colleges require a student who has completed any college-/university-level coursework outside of the United States, even if they are a U.S. citizen or a permanent resident, to complete a supplemental foreign credential evaluation.

Some schools will require you to take the SAT or ACT for admission into certain programs or for scholarship consideration. You will also need to provide colleges with verification of your proficiency in English. An official report of your scores from either the Test of English as a Foreign Language (TOEFL) or the International English Language Testing System (IELTS) should be sent directly to the admissions office of the school to which you are applying.

Note that application deadlines may differ for international students.

Transferring Within the United States

Students transferring from one school to another school within the United States must carefully follow certain procedures to maintain lawful F-1 or J-1 status.

Instructions for Transferring as an F-1 Visitor

Before you can transfer to another school, make sure the school you want to attend is certified by the Student and Exchange Visitor Program. A list of certified schools can be found online at https://www.ice.gov/sevis. Make sure to work on the transfer process with the designated school officials at both your current and new schools.

Once you have been accepted to the new school of your choice, contact that school's designated school official (DSO). To start the transfer process, you'll need the following:

- Written confirmation of acceptance to another Student and Exchange Visitor program (SEVP)–certified school

- Contact information for the new school's DSO

- The Student and Exchange Visitor Information System (SEVIS) school code for the transfer-in school

Then, you will need to work with the designated school official at your current school. Together, you will determine a transfer release date based on your school's academic calendar, your travel plans, and, if applicable, your work situation.

The transfer release date should be the point at which the designated school official at your new school takes responsibility for your SEVIS record. Your SEVIS record must be up-to-date for you to maintain your legal immigration status in the United States, so it is very important that you talk with this official about these matters.

To maintain their legal immigration status, international students need to continue to attend classes while waiting for their transfer release date. Otherwise, your designated school official could terminate your SEVIS record for not abiding by the terms of your student visa.

Once you have a transfer release date, the designated school official at your new school must create a new Form I-20—Certificate of Eligibility for Nonimmigrant Student Status—for you. To maintain your status, register for classes and contact your new DSO within fifteen days of the program start date listed on your new Form I-20.

It's important to note that international students currently employed while studying in the United States cannot continue to work after their transfer release date. Once at your new school, you must talk with your designated school official about obtaining authorization to resume employment.

If you have just arrived in the United States, but you want to transfer to a new school before you begin classes at the school listed on your Form I-20, you must provide the school listed on your Form I-20 with proof—such as an acceptance letter—that you have, in fact, been accepted to the new SEVP-certified school.

Then you will need to report to your new school and enroll in a full course of study within thirty days of arriving in the United States.

Instructions for Transferring as a J-1 Visitor
Individuals who are in the United States with a J-1 status may transfer to another institution in the United States to continue their J-1 program. This means that the research or teaching objective of your stay has to remain the same.

There is no limit on the amount of times a student can transfer, but each time a transfer occurs, it must be approved by the current J-1 program sponsor. Ultimately, any transfer will be allowed at the discretion of the current J-1 sponsor and may be denied for various reasons.

The transfer process is fairly simple. Individuals transferring to another U.S. school do not need to travel abroad to obtain a new J-1 visa sticker at a U.S. Embassy. They will, however, need to communicate their intent to transfer to both their current and new J-1 sponsors, so that the transfer can be executed properly. You should allow a minimum of two weeks for any transfer.

Individuals who are transferring also must not continue their J-1 program at the new institution until the Student and Exchange Visitor Information System (SEVIS) transfer date has been reached and a new DS-2019 form has been issued by the new sponsor. A new DS-2019 form can only be issued by the new sponsor on or after the actual transfer date.

There must be no gap between the end date of activities at the current institution and the SEVIS transfer date to the new sponsor.

MAKING THE DECISION TO TRANSFER

Make sure you're transferring for the right reasons. If transferring wasn't part of your original college plan, start by thinking through all of the aspects of the move. Assess your reasons, and make sure they're compelling enough to make the inconveniences and cost of transferring worthwhile.

PLANNING YOUR COLLEGE TRANSFER

Keep track of the deadlines.
Deadlines vary from school to school. For most schools, begin the application process in October if you want to attend classes during the winter semester. To begin in the fall semester, start the process in January. You will most likely need to send in an application by March or April at the latest if you plan to transfer in the fall.

Check the credit policy.
Colleges have different policies for transfer students. Usually they expect you to have acquired a minimum number of credits. Know what your prospective schools expect, and understand what you'll need regarding courses, credits, and grade point averages. (More on this later.)

Keep up your grades.
Transferring to another college is not like applying to college for the first time. Your college transcripts will be given much more weight than your high school transcripts and test scores. Be prepared to provide transcripts from all of the schools you have attended, including high school.

Measure up to the numbers.
Prepare to measure up to the numbers if you want to transfer to a higher-ranked school. If your high school grades were not high enough, you will need to have made higher grades in college.

Get involved.
Get involved at your current school as if it were your dream school. Colleges look more favorably on students who have taken on leadership roles and activities. You don't want to be seen as a sourpuss who spent their time moping in a dorm room for the past year.

Make connections.
You will likely need recommendations from at least one or two professors. Make connections with professors at your current school.

Explore options.
Approach transferring with your eyes wide open; not all schools are easy to transfer into.

Plan the timing.
Consider waiting until your junior year to attempt a transfer to a highly competitive school. Most colleges provide more open spaces for transfers in that year. Also, you might not have to submit your high

school grades and test scores.

Visit the schools to which you might transfer.
Once you have decided to transfer and have a list of new schools, visit each campus and be sure to sit in on the specific classes that interest you.

You don't want to find yourself transferring again!

COURSE/CREDIT TRANSFER

One of the biggest considerations in a college transfer is the transfer of credits. Don't assume that all of your credits will transfer. Not all classes or credits are transferable, and some schools won't accept credit from a class if you earned lower than a C. Some schools only accept credits for classes that are similar to those they offer. The more specialized the class, the less chance a school will accept the credits.

Know, too, that many colleges set a limit to the number of transfer credit hours they'll allow. You will want to know if you are over the limit. I recommend that you meet with an academic counselor or advisor at the college to which you want to transfer in order to determine which of your credits will likely transfer. Call the school and ask what their policy is regarding this before accepting an admissions offer.

Your best bet is to send a copy of your transcripts to the appropriate department faculty members or admissions advisors and request a credit evaluation in writing. Completing this credit assessment before you move over to your new school can prevent you from taking repeat or overlapping courses and potentially save you a great deal of tuition costs and fees.

For some courses, you may receive elective credit only. This means you may find yourself with enough credits to graduate, but without having fulfilled your new school's general education or major requirements. Make sure you ask specifically how many additional credits you will be required to complete to earn your degree.

As a general rule, your grade point average (GPA) does not transfer. If you transfer, you will most likely start at your new school with a 0.0 GPA. Information on credit transfers can usually be found on a college's website.

If you have one dream school in mind:
If you are planning a transfer before you begin taking classes and you have one dream school in mind as your ultimate goal, ask the appropriate authority at your choice school if they can preapprove courses for credit transfer. See if you can work with that person to set up your course load. However, be sure to keep the door open for the possibility that you'll want or need to finish at your current school; it is best to try to take courses that will work at both schools.

TRANSFERRING FROM A COMMUNITY COLLEGE TO A FOUR-YEAR UNIVERSITY

Some states have articulation agreements between four-year universities and community colleges, and students can check online to see which courses automatically transfer.

More specifically, some community colleges have a dual admissions agreement with certain four-year institutions, in which qualified students can be simultaneously accepted to both schools and then are automatically enrolled in the four-year school after they complete their associate degree at the community college.

Research whether or not your community college has an articulation agreement or a collaborative agreement with the university you'd like to attend. Articulation agreements outline specific courses a university will accept from a two-year institution and they guarantee admission once the two-year curriculum has been completed. Collaborative agreements may not guarantee admission, but they will designate the courses the school will accept as transfers of credit.

ACING THE TRANSFER ADMISSIONS PROCESS

Avoid the following common mistakes in the transfer admissions process:

- Don't miss any deadlines.

- Make sure you send your transcripts to the right office.

Get the right letters of recommendation.
For your transfer application, get recommendations from your college professors. These carry more weight than your older high school recommendations. Approach professors with whom you have a good rapport, especially ones in your academic discipline of choice. If a professor agrees to write a recommendation for you, make sure you thank him or her—verbally before the letter is written, and in writing afterward.

Write the transfer essay.
A transfer essay should present a clear and specific reason why you want to transfer. Good reasons for transferring usually include academic and non-academic opportunities you believe the new college offers. Do not write about love of sports teams, wanting to be near a girl- or boyfriend, or your dislike of your current school. You can mention that your current school isn't a good match for your interests and goals, but be extra-careful not to sound critical, harsh, or bitter.

If you had any problems at your current school, take responsibility for them. As necessary, explain how you plan to improve your performance at the new school.

Schools like to see that you've matured as a person and as a student. Good topics to hit on would include your leadership qualities, your involvement at your school, and your sincere efforts to fit in and make the best of the opportunities you were given. Any time spent attending college should be considered a positive opportunity.

Your essay should also show that you are familiar with and understand the new school to which you are applying. Make sure you research the school well and put relevant details into your essay. If you can replace the name of one college with another, then you haven't written a good transfer essay.

Make sure your essay is error-free before you send it.

ENTERING A DREAM SCHOOL THROUGH THE BACK DOOR

This approach does not have a 100-percent guarantee, but if you desperately want to attend a school and have been rejected as a transfer student, it's worth a try.

Enroll in some evening courses or continuing education credits at your dream school that match courses offered for credit. Your goal here is to accrue approximately forty hours of credit toward your intended major, and then apply to the school as a degree candidate. Note that this can vary depending on the number of credits you already have.

Before you choose to go this route, I recommend that you 1) first apply to the school as a transfer student, and 2) discuss this possibility with your dream school. You should attempt this approach only if you feel good about what you hear.

Chapter 19

Financial Aid,
Including Grants, Loans, and More

In this chapter, I am going to give you an overview of college financial aid and the opportunities that are available. Getting into the details would require an extra book, and many are available just on this subject.

To start off honestly, there is little financial aid for foreign nationals to study in the United States, with the possible exception of citizens of Canada and Mexico. However, over the last decade, there has been a rise in the number of colleges awarding financial aid and the amount awarded to international degree-seeking undergraduate students. This includes both need-based aid and non-need-based aid. Later in this chapter, I list the U.S.-based colleges that award the most financial aid to international undergraduate students.

Most scholarships, grants, and loans from public and private sources are restricted to U.S. citizens. International students do not qualify for federal aid programs, such as Stafford and Perkins Loans or state government scholarships. However, some schools are need-blind, meaning applications are judged solely on their merits, irrespective of a student's ability to pay for tuition, and there are other sources of financial aid that we will discuss.

You can't afford not to go to college. But taking on too much debt and ending up living in your parents' house after college is not your only option. You could become an Olympic champion or a successful entrepreneur. Then you'd get a free ride. Schools love world-ranked athletes, internationally or nationally recognized students, talented musicians, and other students with unique skills, abilities, and backgrounds. Schools also are looking for underrepresented minority students.

Regardless of how much you can pay, we recommend that you don't choose which colleges to apply to solely based on the cost of tuition alone. Schools base financial aid on the difference between the cost and what a family is expected to pay. Before making any decisions, you need to separate the advertised price of tuition and the net cost, which factors in grants and scholarships. Don't make any decisions until after you receive your financial aid award letters and compare them to each other.

While private schools may appear to be more expensive than public schools, most have significant amounts of need-based and merit-based financial aid. You ultimately may find a private school to be less expensive than the public schools that can't provide the aid. Some private schools discount their tuition as much as 50 percent, which reflects their way of competing with other schools. No school wants to lose quality students, if the college can afford it.

Be open to all the possibilities each college offers.

Be realistic, too. Discounts are typically based on a combination of academic merit and financial need. Students with strong high school grades and standardized test scores and high financial need most often receive the best financial aid support.

INTERNATIONAL COLLEGE COUNSELORS TIP:
Look for three categories of assistance in your award letter: gift aid (grants and/or scholarships), work-study job opportunities, and loans. But remember, many financial aid offers are for your freshman year only, and they contain no promises about what your financial aid will look like in future years.

ESTIMATING THE COSTS

Before you send in an acceptance letter, you and your family need to know the bottom line: What is the real cost to attend a school?

All colleges are required by law to post a "net price calculator" on their websites. The net price is an estimate based on the cost of attendance and financial aid policies for the award year. Using the calculator, you should be able to get an idea of the cost of attendance and your eligibility for financial assistance. Once you calculate the real costs, including costs for flights during holidays, you may find that the college that had seemed prohibitively expensive is actually more affordable than you thought.

Keep in mind, however, not all calculators are created equally. The results from the calculators are only estimates, and colleges can calculate them differently, so use them to make rough comparisons between colleges.

THE STUDENT DEBT CALCULATOR

International students will find that there is not a lot of financial aid available for them to study in the U.S. The majority of scholarships, grants, and loans from both public and private sources are usually restricted to U.S. citizens. However, while the options are few, there are ways for international students to get some financial aid and/or scholarships.

In addition to using a net price calculator, make sure you take advantage of the free online financial aid calculator from the U.S. Consumer Financial Protection Bureau. It was created as part of the "Know Before You Owe" initiative. See:
http://www.consumerfinance.gov/payingforcollege.

This online financial aid calculator will give you a better picture of how costs vary at the colleges you're considering, and how much debt you're likely to have after you graduate.

Programmed into the calculator is information on over 7,500 schools. You can enter up to three colleges at a time for comparison. The tool will automatically compare those choices with the national average for schools of their types.

The calculator will show you what your estimated monthly loan payment could end up being, based on the cost of tuition, room and board, books, supplies, other expenses, and the average total amount of grants and scholarships awarded at that particular college.

To make the results more accurate and personalized, you will want to enter your own financial aid information.

To understand the shortcomings of the calculator, make sure you read the detailed explanation of the tool's functions. Keep in mind, the calculator is in U.S. dollars. Estimating the exchange rate for the next four years will not be easy. Also consider currency fluctuations when you calculate a college's costs. Unfortunately, colleges do not adjust their pricing for foreign currency.

ESTIMATING A COLLEGE'S VALUE

The College Scorecard—found at http://collegescorecard.ed.gov—is a planning web tool provided by the U.S. Department of Education. It is designed to provide more information about a college's affordability with regard to its value.

The Scorecard offers information on five key pieces of data about a college: costs, graduation rate, loan default rates, average amount borrowed, and employment following matriculation. These are important elements to consider when choosing a college.

Students and their families start by entering the name of a college of interest or selecting factors that are important to them in their college search.

HOW TO MAKE COLLEGE MORE AFFORDABLE

The most common ways international students can make college more affordable include:

▸ College financial aid: need-based aid and merit aid

▸ Loans

▸ Scholarships

▸ Aid from your home country

▸ Aid from international organizations

▸ Family assistance

In this chapter, I will discuss all the above *except* for scholarships. You'll find everything you need to know about scholarships in chapter 20.

COLLEGE AID: NEED-BASED AID

A number of colleges give financial aid to students from outside of the country. Need-based aid is awarded after a school determines the financial "need" of a student. A financial aid formula is used to calculate the difference between the cost of attending and the amount of money the college believes your family can afford to supply.

Although need-based aid for international students is not common at many colleges, there are some colleges that are "need-blind." At a need-blind college, your application for financial aid will not affect the admission committee's decisions, and, if you are admitted, the school may meet 100 percent of your demonstrated financial need. Some colleges that are need-blind for international students include MIT, Harvard, Yale, Princeton, and Amherst.

Other schools that are "need-aware," but are known for their generous financial aid to international students include Skidmore, Williams, Wesleyan, Trinity, Columbia, Stanford, and Duke. Students should search each of the colleges financial aid websites to see if international students are eligible for need-based aid.

COLLEGE AID: MERIT-BASED

Merit aid, which is awarded on the basis of academic achievement, makes up most of this funding. Merit-based financial aid is awarded by colleges without regard for financial need. Students who receive this type of aid typically have outstanding academic achievements in high school, special talents in the fine arts (music, theater, dance, etc.), excellent athletic skills, or outstanding achievements such as science fair or FIRST competition experience (FIRST Robotics, FIRST Tech, or FIRST Lego).

If you are a student looking for merit aid, here are some tips that can improve your chances of receiving merit aid.

Do research and find the schools that offer merit aid to students. Your best—and most accurate—bet is to search each college's scholarship page on their website. Some publications like *The New York Times* and *U.S. News & World Report* create lists and charts of colleges and universities that award merit aid.

Parents, or students themselves, can also call the school's admissions office or financial aid office and get a general answer on whether a student would be eligible for any merit aid. You do not need to give your name when you call, and you can speak with a representative who can discuss your finances directly—with no cost to you for the trip.

Search https://www.unigo.com/scholarships/merit-based. This is a good starting resource for merit aid.

Choose colleges where you'd be at the top. If your grades and test scores put you in the top 25 percent of the student body, there is a very good chance a school will try to woo you with merit aid.

Take stock of your abilities.
Merit aid also includes athletic achievements and special talents. If you are skilled in sports, music, or another area, merit aid and scholarships focusing on these abilities are worth looking into.

Consider your interests.
Your sports, hobbies, and club involvement may all offer scholarships. Among the countless activities and associations that offer merit aid are beauty pageants, service clubs, religious groups, and honor societies.

Leverage your achievements.
Make a list of the activities you've committed yourself to. There may be merit aid that awards your focused effort.

Evaluate merit-aid scholarships that promote diversity.
You may find you qualify for many merit scholarships simply because of who you are or where you live. A number of schools use merit aid to attract students who are different from the majority of their student body. Qualifications may include being from out of country, being a minority, or even your gender.

See if your major has merit aid.
A number of merit scholarships are earmarked for students who declare a particular major.

Retake the SAT or ACT as necessary.
Higher grades and test scores may generate more aid. A number of schools even state this on their websites.

Apply, apply, apply for scholarships.
These are a form of merit aid under another name. We mentioned a few roads to scholarships previously, but there are literally thousands

of scholarships with all sorts of eligibility requirements.

Negotiate.
If you have received admission letters from two or more schools of equivalent standards, don't be afraid to "bargain." Some schools may be willing to match a merit grant offered by another school.

Although many colleges do not offer merit-based scholarships to international students, there are several that offer partial merit-based scholarships, and even some that offer full tuition merit-based scholarships to international applicants. To be considered for these scholarships, students must complete the specific college's application. Some examples of these schools include: Carleton College, Rice, the University of Miami, Northeastern, and Washington and Lee.

One important thing to note is that the Ivy League schools and some other highly competitive schools *do not* provide merit-based aid. No matter how intelligent, athletically talented, or musically gifted you are, these schools will not give you money based on merit alone.

WORK-STUDY

International student work-study programs provide students with part-time employment at the college to help with college expenses. These programs are typically university-funded work-study programs that provide employment opportunities to students with financial need. The job helps students earn money for educational and personal expenses. Working on campus gives you more flexibility than working off campus, because your campus employers are usually more understanding of class schedules and campus activities. Students may need either an F-1 or a J-1 visa to be eligible to participate.

F-1 and J-1 students may be authorized to work up to twenty hours per week during the academic year and full-time during the summer and official university holiday breaks for on-campus employment. Students

181

who already have assistantships considered to be equivalent to twenty hours a week are not eligible for additional on-campus employment.

At some schools, international students can be hired as an undergraduate teaching assistant (UTA) or as a research assistant (RA), usually during their junior or senior year of college. Both UTAs and RAs generally receive tuition benefits, a stipend, and/or university benefits. An international student applying for a UTA position may have to take a test called the International Teaching Assistant English Evaluation, or the ITA Test.

Keep in mind, international student work-study is different from federal work-study (FWS). Generally, international or foreign students do not qualify for the U.S. federal work-study program.

Students should also keep in mind that school and work can be difficult to manage and they must learn how to balance them.

INTERNATIONAL COLLEGE COUNSELORS TIP:
You can take, reduce, or turn down any part of a college's financial aid offer. You would only do this if it involves a loan or has a "tie," such as a summer obligation, that you don't want to take.

AN OVERVIEW OF LOANS

While grants and scholarships are always desirable, as you don't need to pay them back, the best loan option is different for each family. Loans will need to be repaid with interest. Which loan option is best is determined by your family's unique situation.

It's healthy to have concerns about borrowing money and taking on school loan debt. It's also worth recognizing that it's a viable option to help you achieve your academic goals. It is possible to borrow responsibly and minimize the total amount you'll have to repay.

INTERNATIONAL COLLEGE COUNSELORS TIP:
If a school says that they meet 100 percent of financial need, and it includes loans, they don't mean you will pay nothing. You will need to pay back any loans you are given—with interest.

International students will usually need to have a guarantor or cosigner to enable them to get a student loan. The guarantor/cosigner must be a U.S. citizen or U.S. permanent resident with good credit who has lived in the United States for at least the past two years. This person will be responsible for paying the loan back if you default on your payments. Finding the right cosigner can improve the likelihood of your approval and can also decrease your interest rate.

Different Types of Loans
Let's begin with an understanding of the different types of loans.

There are two main categories of loans: need-based and non-need-based.

Need-based loans are for those students whose families have financial need. These typically have better terms, so consider them first. The lower the interest rate, the less expensive the loan will be and the less you will have to repay.

Non-need-based loans are to help families pay if they can't afford to pay college costs from their current income and savings, or if they would prefer to borrow instead of using available funds.

There are two main types of college loans available for international students: college loans and private loans.

COLLEGE LOANS

Most colleges offer low-interest loans that you don't need to start to pay off until you're out of school. If loans are part of your financial aid package, ask the college about the terms of repayment via email so you can have the answers in writing. Also check out other options so that you can find the best options for you.

Report any private scholarships you earn to your college. Most colleges will subtract the scholarship money from the loans included in your financial aid package, continuing to do so until your loan is gone.

PRIVATE LOANS

I recommend private loans as a last resort. While you can find some with favorable terms, most often the interest rates and fees for these are higher than those for federal loans.

Private loans are generally not subsidized or based on need. While often intended for students, a parent is usually a cosigner, since good credit is often a requirement to get a private loan. If you fail to pay back the loan, your parent/cosigner will be responsible for repaying it.

If you need a private loan, make sure you do a careful comparison. Make sure you understand the interest rate, fees, interest rate capitalization policy, repayment period, prepayment penalties, and any other terms and conditions before you sign anything.

Private education loans are available from banks, schools, and other financial institutions. Again, these loans usually have a higher interest rate than most federal loans.

Some private loans have favorable borrowing terms, but make sure you read everything carefully. (I repeat myself because this is so important!) If there is anything you don't understand, find someone who can explain the details to you.

If you take out any private loans, look for reliable, vetted companies that are approved by the college's financial aid office or have been recommended by a trusted financial advisor.

THE FINANCIAL AID "DON'T" LIST

Don't procrastinate when it comes to financial aid.
Your senior year is not the time to start thinking about making financial aid decisions. Planning financial aid eligibility should start *at the latest* when the student is in tenth or eleventh grade. By getting a head start on understanding the financial aid available and avoiding the most common financial aid mistakes, you can get the best financial aid package possible based on your tentative choices for college. Given the rising cost of college over the years, the tuition for international students at public colleges can be on par with tuition at private colleges.

Keep in mind: The criteria for how public colleges distribute financial aid is very different from the criteria for private colleges.

Don't miss the deadlines.
Make sure you keep track of all deadlines, and don't wait for the last minute here, either. Excuses of technical difficulties and "acts of God" typically fall on deaf ears at financial aid offices. If you miss a deadline, you may eliminate yourself from receiving aid.

Don't base the financial aid you may or may not receive on the aid that any friends did or did not receive.
Each financial aid eligibility situation is entirely unique.

Don't assume that you are eligible for 100 percent of tuition-covering aid.
Even if you're the class valedictorian, the captain of the football team, an oboe player, and a science fair winner, it is unrealistic to expect 100 percent coverage from financial aid packages.

Don't count on your relatives to pay for your tuition.
Unexpected circumstances come up, even for wealthy relatives. So even if a relative has agreed to pay for your tuition, still apply for financial aid. If your relatives do come through, their money can help you pay off your financial aid debt.

185

Don't respond to a college's offer too soon.
Wait until you get in all the financial aid packages from all of the schools to which you have been accepted. Your best leverage for a better financial aid deal is a competitive package from a similar-caliber school. Their aid package could be used to bargain for a better deal from the school you prefer.

Don't try to figure out loans and financing on your own, unless you have to.
It's best to have help when it comes to something as complicated as loan computation. Before securing a loan on your own, seek out an expert whose counsel you can trust. You can also call the college to speak with a financial aid representative who can explain the details to you.

Don't be afraid to borrow if you need to.
Sometimes the college experience that's right for you requires taking some small financial risks. If you're serious about college and you can set—and stick to—your goals, it's a wise investment. You're investing in your future.

INTERNATIONAL COLLEGE COUNSELORS TIP:
Don't take out more loans than you have to. Loans should only be used for unavoidable expenses, such as tuition and fees, room and board, travel expenses, and perhaps books. A career-building summer internship or a fellowship may also qualify as a good reason for a loan. Consider your potential starting salary in your chosen field before borrowing any money. Also consider whether or not you will need to attend grad school. You don't want to spend all your money on your undergrad schooling.

ALTERNATIVE COLLEGE COST-CUTTING MEASURES

Start with an associate degree.
For students with their hearts set on an elite, expensive school, your best bet may be to attend an affordable school first, like a community

college. Credits earned at these less-expensive schools can often be transferred to other universities—even the priciest. Spending two years at a community college can therefore cut your total tuition in half. Your first two years is usually made up of core classes you'd be taking anyway. So it's the last two years that really count for the college name on the diploma. (Read more about transferring—the pros, processes, and pitfalls—in chapter 18.)

Get your college credits for less.
To save time and money, consider shaving a year off of your undergraduate studies.

There are a number of ways you can earn college credits more inexpensively. Take Advanced Placement, A-Levels, or International Baccalaureate courses while in high school, or obtain college credits through the College-Level Examination Program (CLEP). See chapter 8 for more information on AP courses and the CLEP.

Some three-year degree programs have existed for several years at a number of schools, including Bates College in Maine, Lynn University in Florida, and Ball State University in Indiana.

Make sure you read chapter 18 concerning the transferring of credits.

Graduate in four years.
Surprisingly, most students don't graduate on time. If you graduate on time, you'll save on a fifth or sixth year of college costs.

Attend a school with a four-year price guarantee.
Some schools offer guarantee plans that promise the same rate for four years. This guarantee protects students from tuition and fee hikes. Schools that have offered this guarantee include the University of Illinois, Columbia College in Missouri, and George Washington University in Washington, D.C.

Other schools guarantee that their students will graduate in four years. If they don't, the school promises to pay the tuition bill for the next year. Schools that have offered this four-year guarantee include Juniata College, California State Polytechnic University, Green Mountain College, and Western Michigan University.

Become a resident advisor or an international peer advisor.
Students who possess certain social skills can apply to become a resident advisor (RA) or an international peer advisor (IPA). Basically, you become a student supervisor, peer advisor, and/or role model for students who are living in the dorm. RAs usually receive a room for free, as well as other benefits.

Work at a college.
Many colleges offer tuition remission to their employees. This means that if you work at a school for a certain amount of time, you can receive a discount on your tuition. This is also a way to attend a college you might not have gotten into via the regular application process. Several people I know were able to attend prestigious schools because they worked there.

Ask for more financial aid.
At some private colleges, you can negotiate on price. It doesn't always work, but it's worth a try. If you decide to do this, know the terminology the college uses. Some prefer the term "appeal." If you choose to ask a school for more financial aid, don't be surprised if they say no, though, especially if the school is a competitive one.

Steps in "appealing" for more aid:
- Honestly evaluate whether or not you have received a good financial aid offer. If it's a good offer compared to what the school typically gives, you most likely won't get much more aid.

- Think about the support for your case. Consider why you need more aid. Construct a compelling argument for your need for more financial aid.

- Write an appeals or special circumstances letter. Honestly and straightforwardly, clearly outline why you need more financial aid and how you think the school can help you meet your financial needs. Appeals work best if they are based on a change in your family's financial circumstances since the time when you first applied for aid. Possibilities include job loss or other reduction in income, new health expenses, the death of a parent, the disability of a family member, nursing home costs, natural disasters, or parental credit problems that make borrowing impossible.

- Wait. The college needs time to respond.

- Evaluate the results of your appeal.

The worst that can happen is that the financial aid office says no.

INTERNATIONAL COLLEGE COUNSELORS TIP:
Apply to a financial "safety school." This is a school that you and your family can afford without making giant sacrifices.

THE AWARD LETTER

Each school has its own financial aid award letter. Some of these letters are comprehensive and helpful. Others are quite confusing. At times, the letters can even be misleading.

The U.S. Department of Education has been promoting a standard format for all colleges to use, but this is not mandatory yet.

Make sure you fully understand your financial aid package before you accept and sign anything. It is worth seeking help, as needed.

Questions to Consider:
- Does the award letter state whether the school is able to meet your full financial need?

- Is the school offering scholarships, grants, loans, and/or work-study programs?

- How much of the money must be repaid?

- How much will you be responsible for paying now?

- Will you need a private loan?

- Will you be able to afford the debt at a higher interest rate?

- What is the expected exchange rate you are facing ahead?

Chapter 20

Scholarships

GET FREE MONEY FOR COLLEGE!

Students from countries outside the United States can find scholarships to attend American schools. It's not an easy task to find international scholarships because there are so few of them available, but it's not impossible if you put in the effort.

Scholarships pay off in more ways than just free money. They also look impressive on your college applications. Keep in mind, too, you may not get your student visa unless you're able to show how you plan to finance your education in the United States.

What makes scholarships most attractive is that you don't need to repay the money. They're like money trees.

However, even if money grew on trees, you'd still have to work to get it with a ladder and a basket. The same goes for scholarships. They don't come to you. You have to go out and get them. The good thing is that they do exist—many more than there are trees that grow money.

The first step is finding the right scholarships for you. The second step is applying for them. The earlier you start your search, the more likely you are to find and win the scholarships you desire.

Here's a firsthand story about the secret to getting a scholarship, which is *applying* for a scholarship. At International College Counselors, we have a scholarship for ninth-, tenth-, and eleventh-grade students, both in the United States and abroad, which we publicize as widely as we can. And because we work in a high school, we are at least ensured that over five hundred students within a certain region know about our scholarship. One year, we received *one* application from that school's

191

region. When a student I did not know approached me in the hall to see if she had won the scholarship, I was able to confidently congratulate her on her win! How did I know she had won? I figured if she had asked, she had been our one and only applicant!

To apply for our scholarship, visit http://www.iccscholarship.com.

A SCHOLARSHIP OVERVIEW

Scholarships may be available from a variety of sources, including your local or national government, and private sources such as employers, corporations, professional associations, and educational institutions.

Some scholarships are based on financial need. Others are awarded to students with special abilities, qualified as academic, artistic, or athletic achievement. Still more are reserved for people who choose to study in a certain field or who have certain religious affiliations, ethnicities, nationalities, memberships, hobbies, medical conditions, disabilities, or special interests. Some scholarships, like the one offered by International College Counselors, require an essay. Others require illustrations, videos, posters, poems, or unusual last names. The list goes on and on.

In other words, you don't necessarily have to be financially needy to get a scholarship. Nor do you have to have stellar grades.

INTERNATIONAL COLLEGE COUNSELORS TIP:
U.S. citizens who live abroad are eligible for federal and school scholarships.

WHERE TO START YOUR SCHOLARSHIP SEARCH

International students should start their scholarship search in their home country. As mentioned before, scholarships may be offered by government agencies, as well as private sources such as employers, corporations, professional associations, local business organizations, charitable foundations, and educational institutions.

Students don't have to look any further than their computer to find scholarships for which to apply.

Search for scholarships using a web search engine.
Include the keywords "international" and "scholarships" in your search engine and see what comes up. Or use the name of your country and then the word "scholarships." Check Twitter for #scholarship and #scholarships.

Check out the free scholarship databases.
Several free scholarship databases are available online, offering millions of different scholarships worth billions of dollars. Most general scholarship websites do not list the scholarships or they have very limited listings for international students, but a few that do include:

- **Cappex**
  Free online scholarship search service.
  http://www.cappex.com

- **College Board**
  Free online source for scholarships, grants, and loans for college-bound students, including international students wishing to study in the U.S.
  https://bigfuture.collegeboard.org/scholarship-search

- **FastWeb**
  Free online scholarship search service.
  https://www.fastweb.com

- **International Education Financial Aid**
  Free online scholarship search specifically for international students.
  https://www.iefa.org

- **International Scholarships**
  Free online scholarship search specifically for international students.
  https://www.internationalscholarships.com

- **Mobility International USA**
  Free online scholarship resource specifically for international students, including those with disabilities and from developing countries.
  http://www.miusa.org/resource/tipsheet/fundingtous

- **Unigo**
  Free online scholarship search service.
  https://www.unigo.com/

HOW TO APPLY FOR SCHOLARSHIPS—AND MORE PLACES TO LOOK FOR THEM

Applying for a scholarship is a lot like applying for college. There are a lot of choices that you must make in order to put together a list of worthwhile scholarships to spend your time applying for.

Start early.
The more time you put into looking for scholarships, the more choices you'll have. You will also need time to request necessary information and get your materials together. Scholarship requirements may include:

- Transcripts translated into English

- Financial aid forms

- Essays

- Letters of recommendation

- Standardized test scores

- Proof of eligibility, such as a birth certificate

Start small.
Local scholarships are easier to win than ones that draw a national applicant pool. Contact your guidance office and check the scholarship search engines listed above. Type in the name of your city or country into a search engine like Google and then pair it with the word "scholarship" or "scholarships." Or type in the names of your parents' employers, organizations, religious institutions, corporations, and other businesses, and then pair them with the word "scholarship."

Look for scholarships that fit you.
Are you from a developing country? What is your religion? Are you Christian, Jewish, Catholic, Muslim, or an atheist? What about medical conditions? Have you been diagnosed with asthma, diabetes, or multiple sclerosis? If you've answered yes to any of these questions, there may be a scholarship available for you. The more specific the eligibility requirements, the fewer people will apply.

Start looking in your home country.
A number of countries offer scholarships for students seeking to study in the U.S. A few examples of these programs include:

- **King Abdullah Scholarship Program (KASP)** – This scholarship for Saudi Arabian students includes full tuition coverage, health insurance, a monthly stipend, and annual travel to and from Saudi Arabia. In addition, students can receive even more benefits for academic achievements.

- **Brazil Scientific Mobility Undergraduate Program (BSMP)** – This program provides scholarships to undergraduate and graduate Brazilian students to study at U.S. colleges in the fields of Science, Technology, Engineering, and Mathematics (STEM) for one academic year, including a summer internship. Students return to Brazil to complete their degrees.

Seek out international aid organizations.
International humanitarian organizations that promote cultural exchanges between the United States and other countries of the world,

195

such as the United Nations and the World Health Organization, may offer scholarships. Check their websites.

Search for scholarships in your field of study.

If you know what you'd like to study in college—for example, agriculture, economics, hospitality, or health—type those keywords into an Internet search engine along with the word "scholarship." You may be pleasantly surprised. Do this once a week. Not all scholarships appear at the same time.

Check out the unusual scholarships.

Scholarships can also come with unusual eligibility requirements. There aren't many of them, but it doesn't hurt to see what may be out there. Start by typing "unusual college scholarships" into your search engine. Then use keyword combinations to match your specific specialties with the word "scholarships." A few examples of the more esoteric scholarships out there include:

- The Tall Clubs International Scholarship: for women in the United States and Canada who are at least five-foot-ten and men who are at least six-foot-two

- Zolp Scholarships: for students at Loyola University who are Catholic and whose last name is Zolp

- The STARFLEET Academy Scholarship: several scholarships for active members of the Starfleet Academy. (You need to be a member for at least a year.)

- Create-A-Greeting-Card Scholarship Contest: for students who can create a Christmas card, holiday card, birthday card, or all-occasion greeting card.

Check each specific college's scholarship offerings.

For international or undocumented students, your best source of scholarships (and financial aid) will be the college you choose to attend. Although not all, some colleges have scholarship programs specifically for non-U.S. citizens.

196

If you don't live in the United States, you can look at a college's website to see what aid is available to international students. A number of colleges award scholarships to foreign students to help build a student community that is culturally, economically, socially, and geographically diverse. Check to see whether your chosen school has such a program and what requirements are needed to apply for the scholarships. Each school has different funding. Some set aside money for students from specific countries, some are open to students worldwide, and some require that you study in a certain field.

Several U.S. colleges that offer scholarships for international students are listed in chapter 19. There are several others, though, so check each school's policy. Once again, remember that none of the Ivies and only several of the more competitive schools distribute merit scholarships for domestic or international students; it is all need-based financial aid.

If you have exceptional athletic skills, look at the requirements for sports scholarships on each college's website. Apply for these if you are eligible.

If you are confused about the money for which you qualify, call the college and ask to speak with a college admissions officer or financial aid expert.

Don't obsess about the big-money dream.
Ideally you'd get all of your tuition paid with one big scholarship. But realistically, the prestigious, big-money scholarships receive more than 50,000 applications each year. The more money attached to the scholarship, the more well-known the scholarship will usually be. However, if you are truly qualified to be in the running for even the most competitive of scholarships, don't let the opportunity pass you by. Go for it.

Look for "renewable" scholarships.
A US $500 renewable scholarship may not sound like much at first, but over four years, it totals US $2,000.

Determine whether or not you are a realistic candidate.
Don't waste your valuable time. Carefully filter scholarships during your search. You should only apply to the ones that match your skills, heritage, citizenship status, or other qualifications. Scholarships are very strict on these issues.

Apply to only one or two scholarships at a time.
Make your scholarship search more manageable. Give one or two scholarships your all before moving on to the next ones. If you spread your efforts too thin, it will show. This does not mean you should apply for only two scholarships. Set a goal. Give yourself two weeks for two scholarship applications, and then move on to the next.

Do the research.
See who has won the scholarship in the past and make it your job to understand why. You cannot copy what they have done, but chances are, similar entries will also succeed. If you are falling far short of what the past winners offered the scholarship committee, then the scholarship is likely not for you. For example, you will not win a scholarship based on community service if you only have a small amount of volunteer work on your résumé.

Stay organized.
Make separate folders for each scholarship and keep track of what is needed. Track the scholarships on a calendar and make triple sure that deadlines aren't missed.

YOU HAVE A SCHOLARSHIP APPLICATION. NOW WHAT?

Follow the instructions *carefully*.
Follow instructions to the letter. Count the words in the essay and provide the right materials. If you have any questions about what the scholarship requirements are, or how to fill out any part of the application, call or email the scholarship sponsors. Many applications are automatically eliminated because the directions were not followed to the letter.

Stay on topic in the essay/video.
If the essay asks for the philosophical themes of an Ayn Rand novel, don't be clever by comparing her to Batman. Give them what they asked for. Don't give more. Don't give less. Make sure any scholarship application materials or correspondence positions you as someone worthy and deserving of the scholarship.

Check and recheck and recheck the application.
Words must be spelled right and all the questions answered. Make sure it's signed and dated by the right people—for example, by a teacher if that is what the application requests. And make sure all the words can be easily read.

Send the application in on time.
Make sure you do this!

LAST-CHANCE SCHOLARSHIPS

Life is full of surprises, and there are students who will back out of their commitment to a school. This usually happens during the summer, before college starts.

Occasionally, the financial aid set aside for these students will be redistributed. If you want to put yourself in the running to receive these funds, you must be proactive.

Contact your chosen schools in late June or July. This is when they'll be able to tell you just how much, if any, financial aid there is left for the taking.

Research scholarship options.
The rules applying to the disbursal of one scholarship may be different from those of another, even at the same school. Determine which of the school's scholarships that you might be qualified for and call the financial aid office to see which ones might still be available late in the

summer.

Sell yourself.
Be sure to point it out if you boosted your grade point average (GPA) during the latter half of your senior year, a time when many students ease up on doing well.

Be extremely nice.
Being polite and professional can't guarantee that you'll receive funding, but doing the opposite will almost certainly guarantee that you won't see an extra dime.

Try again later.
You never know who will be transferring, dropping out, or kicked out for behavioral or academic issues. The winter is a good time to check back again.

SCHOLARSHIPS DO AFFECT FINANCIAL AID PACKAGES

Contact the financial aid office of any colleges you are considering to find out the details. Each school has its own policy on which types of aid may be reduced or eliminated by the scholarship money. Different types of aid that may be affected by scholarship monies are loans, work-study offers, and need-based grants. But please don't use this as a reason not to apply for scholarships. Here's why:

▸   It's usually best to take whatever you can get!

▸   Scholarship "awards" (and the fact that you won them) are prestigious and look good on college applications.

Beware of scholarship scams.

▸   If it sounds too good to be true, it probably is.

▸   Never pay an application fee.

▸   If you are considering a legitimate scholarship site or scholarship, you will not be asked to pay any money to apply or receive details about the scholarship. The fee can be as low as US $5, but still—don't pay it.

Look up the organization offering the scholarship.
Scams often misuse the names of legitimate government and nonprofit organizations. They may also be using words like "national," "federal," "foundation," or "administration." A website with a ".org" suffix (which is typically used for nonprofit organizations) does not make a scholarship automatically legitimate.

Don't get taken.
If you receive unsolicited mail telling you you've won a scholarship, but you need to send money to claim it, throw the letter away. You won't get thousands, but you will lose money. Another scam will send a check made out to you. In order to cash that check, they will say you need to send them money. Don't send them any money—you won't see any money from them.

Don't pay for what you can get free.
Some scholarship-matching services claim they will help match you with scholarships—for a fee. Before you sign on, do a search of your own for free at sites like http://www.fastweb.com
and http://www.finaid.org
and via Google and Twitter search engines. Many of the paid matching services will send you a list similar to those you can find yourself. Check the free scholarship sites first.

INTERNATIONAL COLLEGE COUNSELORS TIP:
If a scholarship-matching service "guarantees" success or scholarships, don't use it. No one can guarantee you will get a scholarship, so don't pay anyone who says they can *guarantee* that you get one.

Signs of a Scam:
- Mention of high success rates or "free money"
- No website or telephone number

▸ A post-office box used as a return address

▸ Time pressure for a quick reply

▸ Notification by phone

The Sales Pitch That's Not a Scholarship

"Congratulations on being nominated to attend the National Young Leaders Conference in Washington, D.C.," reads the fancy script on the expensive-feeling card complete with gold seal. The card promises a "lifetime advantage" and valuable résumé padding. It's hard to miss the words "elite," "college," "distinguished," and "select."

The letter's claim that this program is a huge honor and that it will distinguish you as a college applicant is simply not true. These particular leadership conferences won't enhance your college applications any more or less than the art club you joined at your high school.

You may meet other kids there who are interested in government, attend workshops, hear speakers, and sightsee, but getting invited isn't an "honor." College admissions officers and college advisors are aware that attendance for most students depends on their home address and their ability to pay.

Companies in this business include/have included: The National Student Leadership Conference, Leadership Classroom, Envision, and the Congressional Youth Leadership Council.

Chapter 21

Free and Inexpensive Schools

International students might be thrilled to learn that a free or very reduced-price college education is available from some very unique colleges, both with a campus and online. A number of them offer free tuition regardless of a student's financial situation, and they accept international students. Some examples of these schools include:

Deep Springs College: http://www.deepsprings.edu/home
Deep Springs offers an associate degree in the liberal arts. Each student attends for two years and receives a full scholarship valued at over US $50,000 per year. The first eligibility requirement for international students is a solid knowledge of English. The school is exceptionally small with a student body that fluctuates between 24 and 30. Only 10 to 15 students per year are admitted. Deep Springs operates on the belief that manual labor and political deliberation are integral parts of a comprehensive liberal arts education. Students of the college work each day on the school's cattle ranch, alfalfa farm, and garden in California's High Desert region.

College of the Ozarks: http://www.cofo.edu
College of the Ozarks focuses on providing a free Christian education to good students who demonstrate financial need. The college was founded to serve students specifically from the Ozarks region, though it occasionally admits students from outside the region, including international students. The school is located in Point Lookout, Missouri.

Full-time students must work 15 hours each week at an assigned campus workstation, which can include a hotel, computer center, fire department, water treatment plant, cafeteria, pool, fruitcake and jelly kitchen, grist mill, museum, theater, or radio station.

Alice Lloyd College: http://www.alc.edu
At Alice Lloyd College, tuition is guaranteed to full-time students. These students must work from 10 to 20 hours each week in a variety of work areas as a condition for graduation. Alice Lloyd emphasizes the integration of Christian principles in every aspect of campus life. Because the college was founded to serve students from the Appalachian region of the United States, only a limited number of international students are admitted. The eastern Kentucky campus is located in the center of Appalachia.

Berea College: http://www.berea.edu
Students admitted to Berea receive a four-year tuition scholarship that covers 100 percent of tuition costs for four years of enrollment. International students are encouraged to apply. Laptop computers are provided to every enrolled student. One of the admission requirements is financial need. The campus is located in Berea, Kentucky.

Lynn University's Conservatory of Music:
http://www.lynn.edu/academics/colleges-schools/conservatory
Lynn University's Conservatory of Music provides full-tuition scholarships to students regardless of their financial situation or citizenship. Admissions are based on artistic promise. Bachelor of Music specializations include study of applied instrument, chamber music and/or large ensemble, music history, music theory, and Lynn University's nationally recognized Dialogues core curriculum. Performance requirements include juries, mock orchestral auditions, and junior and senior recitals. Additional course requirements vary based on what you choose to study. Students who are unable to do a live audition can submit a video through Acceptd. No other form of video audition will be accepted. The web link for Acceptd is https://app.getacceptd.com/lynn.

Webb Institute: http://www.webb.edu
Webb offers one academic option: a double major in naval architecture and marine engineering. Located in Glen Cove, New York, it's a full-tuition scholarship private program open to international students. In

204

addition to the full-tuition scholarship, Webb students are eligible to apply for additional school scholarships.

Franklin W. Olin College of Engineering: http://www.olin.edu
Every admitted student receives a half-tuition merit scholarship valued at more than US $80,000 over eight semesters. Admission to Olin is need-blind. The school is located in Needham, Massachusetts.

Western Governors University: http://www.wgu.edu
WGU is an online university that charges tuition at a flat rate every six months, so you pay for the time, not the credit hours. If you can complete your program in less time by taking more classes in any given semester, you only pay tuition for the time it takes. In other words, the faster you progress, the more money you can save.

Chapter 22

Tips for High School Student Athletes

A number of colleges offer priority admissions and athletic scholarships to students who are very talented in a particular sport. The gifted athlete's top question is: How do I get recruited by an American university?

My answer: An athlete needs to get noticed by the right school and the right coach. This means the ones that fit your needs and abilities.

First, the bad news. When it comes to sports scholarships, high school student athletes in the United States have an advantage over international students. In the United States, talented student-athletes may have had some exposure to college coaches at local, regional, and national competitions. In the United States, high school coaches may also have contacts with university program coaches and scouts. Scouts may also be tracking the progress of talented U.S. high school athletes in the news and/or at sports competitions.

The good news is that every year talented international student-athletes are successful in receiving scholarships in a variety of sports at a wide range of U.S. schools. And although some schools, including the Ivy League schools, do not offer sports scholarships, many schools, including highly competitive colleges like Stanford University, Duke University, and UCLA, do.

Sports scholarships are granted by the university's athletic department. Athletic directors and coaches play a central role in award decision-making. Scholarships are generally awarded for the following sports: baseball, basketball, crew (rowing), cross-country, fencing, field hockey, football (American), football/soccer, golf, gymnastics, ice hockey, lacrosse, skiing, softball, swimming and diving, tennis, track and field, volleyball, water polo, and wrestling.

The reality is that even in the United States, high school coaches do not always help their athletes to get scholarships. Many of them don't have the time or the resources. Many times, if a U.S. student wants a college scholarship and other athletic opportunities, they must do a lot of work on their own. The steps to the international college sports recruiting process are similar to the steps in the United States college sports recruiting process, as far as getting recruited. The main difference is in the technicalities.

Get competitive and keep your eye on the prize. International student-athletes need to start working on their recruitment process early. Start developing your own networks, resources, and contacts for recruitment as early as you can.

Scholarships are provided on a yearly basis, generally renewable for four years, the normal time required to complete an undergraduate degree. Renewing a scholarship is up to the coach's discretion. Award amounts vary and can be anywhere from a few thousand dollars to a full scholarship.

Students with sports scholarships must be earning an undergraduate degree at the university and meet the academic standards for the sports program and/or scholarship.

HOW TO GET RECRUITED

Learn the athletic association's recruiting rules and eligibility requirements.
To get started, research the athletic associations and eligibility requirements for your sport to determine the programs that best suit your academic goals and professional ambitions. Athletic associations govern college sports and set the rules for sports scholarships and athletic recruitment. The main associations linked to high-level college sports are:

▸ National Collegiate Athletic Association (NCAA)—The NCAA

207

counts over 1,200 colleges, universities, conferences, and organizations as its members. It administers 23 sports. Members are classified within three NCAA divisions (Division I being the most competitive). Only students with the very highest standard of ability tend to be recruited.

▶ National Association of Intercollegiate Athletics (NAIA)—The NAIA is a smaller association of schools than the NCAA. Each year approximately 60,000 student-athletes play college sports at one of the 240+ NAIA member institutions. The association sponsors 14 sports and conducts 25 annual championships. Most NAIA institutions offer scholarships to student-athletes.

▶ National Junior College Athletic Association (NJCAA)—The NJCAA governs two-year college athletics. There are three divisions, with scholarships offered at the Division I and II levels. Division I colleges may offer full scholarships, and Division II may offer partial scholarships. Division III schools do not offer sports-related financial aid.

Register with the NCAA Eligibility Center.
College-bound student-athletes preparing to enroll in a Division I or Division II school need to register with the NCAA Eligibility Center to ensure they have met initial eligibility standards. The Eligibility Center can be found on the NCAA website at NCAA.org.

Watch this video: http://www.freerecruitingwebinar.org
The Free Recruiting Webinar, operated by the 501(c)(3) nonprofit Recruiting Education Foundation, Inc., is designed to educate athletes and parents on the recruiting process. In approximately one hour, it addresses many important recruiting topics, including scholarship myths and facts, the NCAA and NAIA eligibility centers, NCAA core course requirements, national letters of intent, finding the right school, and much more.

Identify schools of interest.
Research colleges and their sports programs. Read about the teams and

look into a few players' profiles to determine the general level of needed athleticism. Also research the qualifications and reputation of the coaches and programs. You will also want to look into the reputation of the university and your program of study. Other things to consider include academic strength, level of athleticism, geographic location, and the size of the school. See chapter 14 for more information on creating a school list.

Contact the coaches.
Depending on your sport, start contacting coaches at schools of interest and building relationships with them as early as possible. The goal is to get coaches and recruiters to know your name in a good way. For example, send them some newspaper articles about you and the teams you play for, or a link to a particularly spectacular achievement. If there is an opportunity to meet a coach, go and introduce yourself with a quick rundown of your best achievements. You may ask them the best way to showcase your talents. Some will request videos; some will have camps; some will want a sports résumé. Learning early what is needed is the key to meeting the coach's needs.

One thing to note is that although you may contact a coach anytime you want, coaches are not allowed to call or email you back until the end of your junior year. If you contact a coach and the coach happens to pick up the phone, then the coach can talk to you. Realize, though, that coaches are extremely busy and many get hundreds of calls, so this does not frequently happen. Some coaches have designated days and times for athletes to contact them, so check to see if this is the case with the coach whom you're trying to contact.

Create a sports résumé.
Highlight your athletic and academic achievements. Keep track of all your meets, tournaments, and achievements to display on the résumé. Specifically, you will want to write down the following:

▸   The teams you have played for and the positions you have held

▸   All your statistics, including goals, hits, assists, blocks, runs, or whatever else is measured in your sport

▸ Your best times, heights, scores, etc., if you're an athlete who competes in a sport with a matrix, like track and field, cross country, swimming, or bowling

▸ Your individual and team's wins and losses

▸ Any awards you've received, including Most Valuable Player (MVP), Most Improved, Scholar Athlete, Defensive Player of the Year, etc.

▸ Any extracurricular experiences you've had in your sport, such as coaching a junior league

Make a sports video of yourself in action.
This direction is for athletes who compete in sports without a measurable matrix. There is a real probability that a college coach will never have the opportunity to see you play in real life until you play for him or her. The best video would be a combination game video and skills video. You want to keep it relatively short (about five minutes) and put your best highlights first. Don't forget to include your contact information—your name, school, phone number, email address, and coach's name, and email address. Consider setting up a channel for yourself on YouTube and then sending the link to coaches. You can also post your video on an athletic recruiting website.

Get into the Internet zone.
Visit college sports sites and college websites and collect as much information about the different sports programs as you can. You're looking for a school that will be a good fit for you and your talents, both athletically and academically.

Get evaluated (if you can).
Many third-party people serve as the eyes and ears of the coaches who don't have time to get out and see every player. Get to know the evaluators in your area. Coaches and evaluators face immense pressure to fill their slots with the most gifted athletes they can find. Their jobs depend on it. Your proactivity actually can make their job easier from

210

their perspective.

Involve your high school coach.
Approach your current or former coach and ask if they will follow up with the college coaches for you. College coaches cannot respond to your phone calls and emails until the end of your junior year, and they oftentimes are not available to take your calls when you contact them, but a college coach can return a call to your club or high school coach, who can then organize a time for you to talk. They can also help to write letters of recommendation to support your applications.

Attend college sports camps (if you can).
The director of the camp will usually be the college head coach. Take these camps seriously and use them as opportunities to showcase your talents.

Make yourself academically eligible.
Potential recruits need to qualify for admissions to the college at which the athletic program is offered. This means reaching a certain minimum grade point average (GPA) and/or standardized test score. No matter how athletically gifted you are, most colleges still require a minimum GPA and/or standardized test scores. You should also plan to take the SAT or ACT early, so coaches can know whether they should consider you.

Keep up your grades.
With the exception of big-time college men's American football, men's and women's basketball, and women's volleyball, other sports do not typically offer full athletic scholarships for budgetary reasons. However, many colleges do offer what is called merit money. This is where academics come into play. If you have good grades, a college can offer you a half-athletic scholarship as well as a half-merit scholarship based on your grades. This can equal a full scholarship.

INTERNATIONAL COLLEGE COUNSELORS TIP:
If a college does show interest in you, answer any request they may

211

have immediately. If a coach or school is requesting more information, chances are you are probably being seriously considered. Ask your high school coach to complete any requests for information about you as soon as possible.

OTHER FUNDING OPTIONS

Because athletic scholarships are so competitive, student-athletes may want to explore other options for funding based on special interests and extracurricular activities.

A BRIEF FOUR-YEAR HIGH SCHOOL TIMELINE

Freshmen

Take this year to grow and develop your skills. Look into joining club teams and attend sports camps and clinics to hone your skills. Also, plan your academic calendar. You want to make sure you meet the academic eligibility at the end of your high school career. Even a high school sports superstar will not be eligible to play as a college freshman if he or she does not have a transcript with the right high school courses. Athletes and parents of athletes, make sure you read the *NCAA Guide for the College-Bound Student Athlete*. A free PDF of this guide may be downloaded at https://www.ncaapublications.com/. Students can start their athletic résumé this year and then add to it over time. You should also see if you can get someone to video-record your games/matches/meets so that you can put together a highlight video. Try to recruit a friend or family member to do this for you. The video can also help you to identify your mistakes and improve in the future.

Sophomores

Get serious if you are interested in competing in college. Start working on raising your visibility and building a reputation as a mature, hardworking team player. This is also the year you should start researching the ins and outs of recruiting, regulations, colleges, coaches, and sports programs. Keep up your athletic résumé and continue to

212

have a friend or family member recording your performances at sporting events.

Juniors

This year is your most important one. It is the accomplishments of your junior year that will get the recruiting phone calls later in the year. Talk to your coach about serving as the captain of your team; if it doesn't work in your junior year, you can try again in your senior year. Get on the college coaches' radar screens as soon as possible through proactive emails to better your chances of successfully getting recruited. Boost your visibility by completing online athletic surveys for particular colleges, visiting schools, attending sports camps, and meeting coaches. Don't get discouraged if you don't hear from any coaches. NCAA rules prevent them from contacting or calling you directly until late in your junior year.

Seniors

Make sure that you complete all the classes you need for academic eligibility. Show continuing development in your sports skills. Don't slack off until after you've received and signed the "Letter of Intent"— and even then, if you really mess up, they can drop you, so maintain your level of skill and your grades.

INTERNATIONAL COLLEGE COUNSELORS TIP:
Take care of your body and keep working hard to get stronger, faster, and more fit. It's a competitive environment out there—but if you're a true athlete at heart, knowing that should only help to push you harder.

Chapter 23

Independent College Advisors

Many international families have turned to working with a private college counselor. It's a trend that's been on the rise. As other students you're competing against are hiring independent advisors, I did want to mention what to look out for if you're considering hiring someone for yourself.

Independent college advisors can be of enormous value, if they are used correctly.

VALUE OF INDEPENDENT COLLEGE ADVISORS

Primarily, independent college advisors provide you with the individualized attention you need to properly tackle the college admissions process. This is about you—the individual—and finding the best fit for you.

A good college advisor will help you with your college selection and the application process. Some parts of the admission process include: providing help with high school planning; refinement of extracurricular and academic interests; advice, review, and critique of your essays; interview preparation; exploration of financial aid and scholarships; and wait-list and deferral strategies.

Additionally, independent advisors can help relieve stress and maximize results.

CHOOSING AN INDEPENDENT COLLEGE ADVISOR/ EDUCATIONAL CONSULTANT

Like in any field, there are individuals who are good and others who are not. Many people moonlight as college advisors or consider themselves to be "experts" because they just helped their daughter/son/friend get into their top choice of college. Others have questionable ethical standards.

In choosing an independent college advisor, I recommend looking for these factors:

Professional Memberships

All independent college advisors should belong to at least one professional organization like the National Association for College Admission Counseling (NACAC), the Higher Education Consultants Association (HECA), or the Independent Educational Consultants Association (IECA). These organizations are for serious professionals. For both of these organizations, the member must have at least three years of professional experience, must have worked with multiple students, and must have their application approved by a committee.

Credentials

Review the college counselor's credentials. Does the advisor have a bachelor's degree from an accredited institution? Does the advisor have at least three years of experience as a college advisor? Has the advisor previously placed students in colleges you are targeting? If so, how many and where? If the advisor has only placed students in local, public schools, this may not be a good fit for you. Does the advisor use a web-based college research tool like Naviance to track former students—their grades, scores, and other variables—to compare them to you?

Current in the Industry

Advisors should be meeting with admissions representatives, visiting colleges, going to workshops, reading up on trends, and fully immersed in college admissions. Your English teacher may be an excellent writer and proofreader, but does she really know what's trending on college entrance essays and what the admissions representatives want to see?

Team Approach

With over 4,500 colleges to consider, not every college counselor can

215

know everything about each school. Look for a company that shares resources on schools, admissions strategies, and college contacts. The team approach is also beneficial when it comes time to review essays. Does the company have someone who does a second review? Even the best editors miss mistakes, so it's always better to have a few eyes reading over the essays.

Ethical Standards

College advisors should observe the highest legal and moral standards. A college advisor should not write your college essay, "guarantee" admission into a certain school, or help fabricate information on a transcript. Additionally, similar to how colleges perform Internet searches on students, you should do a search on your advisor or the company. If the first thing that comes up is something about questionable behavior, you may want to look elsewhere.

Time and Communication

Your independent advisor should be available when it's convenient for you, within reason. Are they available after school, on the weekends, and when school is out? Are they available via Skype, phone, and email? Is this their full-time position, or do they merely dabble in college advising?

Location

It is much easier for college advisors based in the United States to visit U.S. colleges, meet with admissions representatives, and communicate with colleges because of the time difference. If you're considering a college advisor from outside the United States, make sure to find out how often they visit U.S. colleges and meet with U.S. admissions representatives, so that they are current on what's going on in U.S. colleges.

QUESTIONS TO ASK INDEPENDENT COLLEGE ADVISORS

Think about what's most important to you when hiring an independent college advisor. This person is going to be helping you to make one of the biggest decisions of your life. Some questions you may want to consider include:

- Do you belong to any professional associations? If so, which ones?

- How do you keep up with trends in the U.S. admissions process?

- How often do you visit U.S. colleges or meet with U.S. admissions officers?

- Do you attend any professional conferences or ongoing training?

- How long have you been in business as an independent college advisor?

- What is your experience in college advising?

- Is college advising your full-time profession?

- Have you placed any students in Ivy League/top-tier schools? If so, which ones?

- At which grade in school do you start working with a student? (You really want one who starts with students beginning in secondary school.)

- Do you work alone, or do you have colleagues with whom you work in a team approach?

- What type of web-based college research tools do you use?

- What type of services do you offer, and how much do you charge for your services?

- Do you offer hourly or comprehensive packages?

- Will you meet or Skype with me initially for free?

- How do you communicate with students? Do you keep parents included in the communication?

- How do you measure a student's success?

You should ask the following additional questions to check for scammers. If they answer yes to any of these, look elsewhere!

- Do you guarantee admission into a school?

- Do you guarantee scholarship money?

- Will you write my college application essay?

- Do you accept any form of compensation from a school in exchange for placement?

- Are there any additional fees other than what is outlined on the contract?

INTERNATIONAL COLLEGE COUNSELORS TIP:
Similar to picking the right college, you want to click with your advisor and make sure he or she understands your goals. We recommend signing up with an advisor who will meet with you first—either in person or virtually—before you sign on the dotted line.

Of course, if you are reading this book and finding it helpful, but want a more personalized approach to getting through the U.S. college admissions process, you should consider working with the expert advisors at International College Counselors. We work with students from all over the world with successful results. We will make the process easier for you from beginning to end. Feel free to visit our website at www.internationalcollegecounselors.com or contact us at info@internationalcollegecounselors.com or +1 (954) 414-9986.

Chapter 24:

The Application Is In.
Don't Relax Yet.

SIGNS, SYMPTOMS, AND DANGERS OF SENIORITIS

Symptoms: Laziness. Skipping classes. Failing to study hard for tests or write coherent papers. Disinterest in school-related academics and activities.

Diagnosis: Senioritis.

Prescription: Graduation.

Senioritis refers to being a senior in your last year of high school. Avoid the epidemic. Don't catch senioritis. Slacking off during your senior year may seem like something you feel you deserve, but chances are you'll do yourself more harm than good.

First, you'll miss out on a half-year's worth of learning. This will leave you less prepared for college.

Second, college admissions officers really do pay attention to what you accomplish in your senior year. They look at your grades and your activities and, in some cases, your more recent social networking posts.

The temptation to blow off school and all the work involved is especially strong when students have already been accepted into college.

But did you notice whether your college application package included a form called the "mid-year grade report"? Your counselor or program coordinator typically fills it out and sends it off to your college of choice when the time comes, and it will become part of your full admissions evaluation.

Colleges do have the right to block your admission, and acceptances can get rescinded. Read your college acceptance letters carefully. Many times colleges include clear warnings to students, informing them that their admission is contingent on successful performance throughout their senior year.

The number of students who have their acceptance offers rescinded is small, as the academic drop usually needs to be significant before colleges go that far. However, colleges can and do punish in other ways. A student may receive a harsh letter warning them to get it together. Or he or she may need to explain, in a letter or a phone call, what has happened with their academic performance. A drop in performance can also result in other consequences such as getting dropped from an honors program or having your admission postponed. These situations are not as rare as you may think.

Generally, the more selective the college, the more weight is put on what you do in your final semester of high school.

INTERNATIONAL COLLEGE COUNSELORS TIP:
We always recommend sending update letters to colleges about a month after your application has been sent in. In this way, you can reiterate your interest, update the school on any new accomplishments, and allow the school to see that you are a serious student.

Don't plan on doing anything stupid, no matter where you plan to go to college. Colleges regularly rescind admissions offers from students who get arrested or suspended from school for unlawful or prohibited activities like drinking.

Don't plan on dropping any courses. Even substituting an online course for one you're taking at school will raise red flags with a college admissions office. Admission offers have been revoked because colleges see a dropped course as significant underperformance, especially if the student drops a rigorous course. It's really not worth it.

My sincere recommendation is to take preventive care. Senioritis may not be curable, but it is treatable: Stay active. Stay involved. Stay focused. Stay on your regular schedule. Take a college course to get yourself more prepared for college. The credit may even count at your college later, and that's one less class you'll need to take.

You have done most of the hard work, and it would be foolish to let all of that hard work go to waste now. You also have a whole summer to goof off, if that's what you really want to do in between filling out the dorm room papers and shopping for beanbag chairs.

Chapter 25

College Responses and Decision-Making

When high school seniors know that college notification dates are near, there is little they can do to feel less anxious. Chances are that moms, dads, counselors, teachers, and even principals are feeling anxious themselves.

Even if you get into your first choice college, this will probably be a hard time for you. You're hardly alone. After the initial euphoria, most students start thinking about what going to college really means.

For students who get rejected, this may be the first time they're having to deal with major disappointment. Don't let this damage your self-esteem. Feel your emotions and think them through.

THE MANY POTENTIAL OUTCOMES OF THE COLLEGE APPLICATION PROCESS

Acceptance/Admittance
Yay! So you've been admitted to the school to start in the fall of the next year, as long as you don't do anything truly drastic. Don't let your grades drop significantly and don't get arrested, among other things. As previously mentioned, schools have the right to withdraw their acceptance. If you have been accepted, you typically have until May 1 to submit your financial deposit to secure your place at the school.

Deferral
A deferral is different than being wait-listed. A deferral means that a student who applied Early Action or Early Decision is being considered as a regular applicant. You've neither been accepted nor denied; your application was simply rolled over into the regular decision pool. Given that the school can only admit a limited number of applicants per

semester, the school wants to compare you to the students who apply for Regular Decision. If you are deferred, it can always help if you show additional interest in the college. See my advice below on how to handle a deferral.

Denial

This means you have not been accepted to the school. Don't take it personally, and read my advice below on your response to the admissions decision.

Wait-List

This means, quite literally, that you're on a wait-list. The schools know you exist, but you're not a first-choice applicant. Whether or not you get off the wait-list and into the school depends on how many of the accepted students decide to attend the school. If you're wait-listed and really want to go to your first-choice college, you may have to make a deposit at another school as an insurance policy. While this is bad for students, wait-lists are good for colleges. Wait-lists allow them to ensure that they have enough students to fill all of their spaces. Send the school any new updates that might later enhance your application.

Conditional Admittance

Select applicants who do not meet the minimum admissions requirements but who show potential for success may get a "conditional admittance." This means the school wants you, but you need to fulfill other requirements before they can fully admit you. If you get one of these letters, the school will let you know what you need to do—for example, complete a summer/special program, or take certain classes during your freshman year of college.

Spring or Summer Admittance

Sometime a student is accepted on the condition that he or she starts classes in a term other than the fall. Students can inquire as to whether the school offers academic options, study-abroad programs, or other opportunities to fill the time gap. Other students use the gap time to take courses at a community college, to work, or to travel. Schools usually do this because there is additional room on campus in the spring and summer semesters, when students study abroad or are on summer break.

Guaranteed Transfer or Deferred Admission
This means that the college recognizes your potential but it doesn't believe your record is strong enough to admit you at the current time. Typically this letter says that if you attend another university for a year and maintain a certain grade point average (GPA), they will then guarantee you a transfer spot in your sophomore year. There are a number of colleges that offer and have offered this option, including Cornell University, the State University of New York System, Middlebury College in Vermont, and the University of Maryland. If you really have your heart set on a certain school, ask about this option. Some colleges do not advertise that they offer deferred admission.

YOUR RESPONSE TO THE ADMISSIONS DECISION

Typically, a deferral means the college wants to compare you with the full applicant pool, because your application did not shine brightly enough for them to admit you early.

Unlike a rejection, a deferral offers hope and a chance. Ironically, hope is not always the least stressful option. You still have work to do if you want to improve your chances of turning a "maybe" into a "yes."

Here are some suggestions:

▸ Don't panic.

▸ If possible, try to determine the reason you weren't accepted straightaway.

Get information.
Contact the admissions office and see if you can learn why you were deferred. Then ask for suggestions regarding turning your deferral into an acceptance. By doing this, you'll make the school aware of your

224

commitment and get more information. Do not call if the college has specifically asked that students not call them, however.

Send in improved standardized test scores.
This is especially important if you believe your submitted scores might not have measured up.

Send in your midyear grades if the college asks for them.
Make sure you meet their deadline. (This is another reason it's important not to let your grades slide.)

Write a letter.
Sincerely express your continued interest in the school and any reasons you believe it would be a good match for you. Do not come across as whiny or negative. Be yourself; sound personal; be interesting; and be positive. Attach information about any new and meaningful accomplishments that are not in your original application. Accomplishments could include new activities, new awards, or leadership positions.

Send in any strong and relevant additional recommendations.
The best letter of recommendation would discuss your unique qualities and why they make you an ideal match for a school. What you don't want to do, however, is send a generic recommendation. Make sure you check to see if the college allows you to send any extra letters before you send them.

Let go.
There is no one "perfect" school. Hope for the best, but prepare to go to one of your backup schools.

INTERNATIONAL COLLEGE COUNSELORS TIP:
At all times while communicating with the college, be polite, concise, professional, positive, and enthusiastic. Don't express frustration or anger or try to convince the school they made a mistake.

DEFERRAL LETTERS THAT WORK BEST

Letters of appeal work best if you can give the college more reasons to reconsider you—for example, a new honor or a significant achievement. Also important to include in the letter would be a few lines that reaffirm your interest in the school. And don't forget to thank the admissions officer!

Sample Deferral Letter 1

Dear Mr. Garcia,

Although my admission for Early Action has been deferred, I am still very interested in Northeastern and would very much like to be admitted, and therefore I wish to keep you up to date on my activities and achievements.

Earlier this month I participated in the National High School Model UN Conference in New York, where I was elected to serve as the Secretary-General. As a part of this position, I was an integral part of the conference logistics and planning, as well as presiding over the conference. At the conference, I spoke to advisors, met people's concerns, managed staff and duties, and made sure everything went smoothly.

I was extremely honored to be chosen based on my strong organizational, leadership and communication skills.

Thank you for your continued consideration of my application.

Sincerely,
Name
High School Country
Application ID

Sample Deferral Letter 2

Dear Ms. Davis,

Last week I learned that my application for Early Decision at Johns Hopkins was deferred. As you can imagine, this news was disappointing to me—Johns Hopkins remains the university I'm most excited about attending. I visited several schools during my college search, and Johns Hopkins's program in International Studies appeared to be a perfect match for my interests and aspirations.

I want to thank you and your colleagues for the time you put into considering my application. Since I applied for Early Decision, I have received a few more pieces of information that I hope will strengthen my application. First, I retook the SAT in November, and my score rose from 1460 to 1510. The College Board will be sending you an official score report soon. Also, I was recently elected to be the captain of our school Ski Team, a group of twenty-eight students who compete in regional competitions. As captain, I will have a central role in the team's scheduling, publicity, and fund-raising. I have asked the team's coach to send you a supplemental letter of recommendation that will address my new role within the Ski Team.

Many thanks for your consideration,
Name
High School Country
Application ID

HOW TO DEAL WITH DISAPPOINTMENT

Talk it out.
If you are rejected from your first choice college, find a trusted adult with whom you can vent your emotions. You need to accept that you didn't get in and move forward with the opportunities that do present themselves. If you have been rejected, some schools do offer opportunities for appeal, but unfortunately, these are rarely successful.

227

While getting into your first-pick college is important, if you don't, it's not the end of the world. You shouldn't love or like yourself any less. College is one step on a long road. Sure, it's a big step, but it's not the final destination.

Add up what really counts.

The college admissions officers are looking at numbers: a grade point average (GPA), an SAT score, and the number of applicants to that school that year. Numbers have little to do with you as a good person. Besides, it's too late now to change the numbers, so beating yourself up isn't going to make anything better.

Remember the subjectivity factor.

Much of the college admission process is out of your control. While I do believe admissions officers try to be fair and thorough, college admissions are subjective, perhaps even more than most students and parents realize. High scores aren't the only thing that counts. Subjectivity comes into play as admissions officers compare the applications. Maybe the band really needed a new bassoon player. Perhaps the school does not need another rhythmic gymnast. Sometimes the numbers just don't work in your favor.

Celebrate the acceptances.

Celebrate the college acceptance letters that you do get. Getting into any college is something to celebrate.

Consider additional applications.

Even as late as April and May, some colleges are still accepting applications. Wish you had applied to a different particular school? Now is the time to see if they still have any openings.

INTERNATIONAL COLLEGE COUNSELORS TIP:

The Common Application allows you to sort applications by deadline. Don't be afraid to apply to colleges even toward the end of your senior year.

Remember that you can always transfer. Our recommendation is to keep this as a back-pocket option and not as a goal. If you start at a college with the intent of transferring, you won't be able to enjoy the full college experience you might otherwise have. Many students find that once they settle in, they're actually very happy where they ended up.

In the meantime, I promise, no matter what happens: After the madness, there will be a calm.

ACCEPTANCE! DECISION-MAKING AFTER THE ACCEPTANCE/REJECTION EMAIL

The emails have been opened, and the web portals have been read.

If you have more than one acceptance in your hand, you're now in the driver's seat. The colleges have taken their sweeeeet time choosing you, and now it's your turn to choose them. They've given you the month of April to make your choice. Far beyond the glossy paper of the brochures, here are some things you should consider:

Economics
It's hard to deny that this may be a factor for many students. If you have been offered a generous financial aid package or a scholarship at a certain school, it is going to be hard to ignore this "bonus." However, the price tag may not be so much a factor in some cases. Some families have the funds, and some schools have the funding. In fact, Ivies and a small number of other schools across the country have policies that will meet the full financial need of students and allow them to attend irrespective of their ability to pay.

What you need to do with any offer is to carefully review it. Look at the tuition and the amount and type of financial aid you were offered. Go back and reread chapter 19 on financial aid.

At many schools, once you are offered admission, as an international student you may be required to submit a certification or a statement of finances, demonstrating that you will be able to fund your four years of study through a combination of your own funds and any financial assistance the college may provide. Make sure to send this in to the college if they are requesting this information from you.

Fit

Where do you feel like you will fit in best? Some students thrive at universities where the city itself plays an important role in one's overall education. Cities included on this list include New York, Boston, New Orleans, and Los Angeles. The cultural and internship opportunities in these places can also be enormous. However, city schools tend to be more impersonal, and cities aren't as conducive to a school community atmosphere. Residential campus schools like Dartmouth College in Hanover, New Hampshire, or Williams College in Williamstown, Massachusetts, pride themselves on providing everything you need right there on campus, from cultural activities to social life. They have more of a community atmosphere.

In order to figure out how you might fit, you should ideally visit the school. It's the only way you'll get a real feel for the location and the culture. On campus, try to speak with both professors and students.

If you can't physically visit, try to talk to current students, recent alumni, or admissions officers.

Academics

Do you have an idea of what you want to do in the future? Ideally, you should have a vague idea of the career path you want to pursue, and you need a school that offers a major or program that will allow you to explore that option to its fullest. For example, if you know you want to go to medical school when you graduate, make sure there's an undergrad program strong in math and science courses.

Also be aware that there can be real differences in the courses of study at various places. Some schools like Columbia University and the University of Chicago require students to take a core curriculum. These mandatory courses can take up to two years to complete. Open curriculum schools, like Brown and Amherst, have no required courses. Instead they require that students take one of a list of first-year seminars. Guidelines and advisors at these schools help students with their course choices.

I also recommend that you research the professors and special opportunities available at different schools. The University of Michigan College of Engineering, for example, creates partnerships between first- and second-year students and UM faculty and research scientists.

Culture
At some schools, like the University of North Carolina, students often feel that the culture revolves around sports. At others it could be around academics, religion, or a certain industry. At the University of Southern California, for example, the entertainment industry seems to have a permanent presence no matter what students are studying. At New York University, the city is a center of life. Some schools have a large international student population and others do not. The key to the culture is the students. Talk to the students. They can tell you what the school is really like. What are the dorms like? What does everyone do on Friday or Saturday nights? Ask a student from your country how easy or hard it has been to fit in.

Job Connections
After college you'll want to get a job, so it's smart to consider a college's career services center. Call them and ask about job fairs, internship opportunities, on-campus corporate interviews, and the number of students per career counselor.

INTERNATIONAL COLLEGE COUNSELORS TIP:
Only you will know what is truly important to you. I suggest you create a list of all the questions you want to have answered and then go visit the school. If you've already visited the schools, then visit your top two choices again. Take a good hard look at each school. Can you see

yourself fitting into the culture? Do you feel comfortable? This is going to be your home away from home for the next four years.

Specific questions you may want to ask if you haven't already: How hard is it to get into the classes I want? How small or big are the classes? Are there internships, and how does the school help students prepare for life after college? Does the school provide career placement or help with graduate and professional programs? Does the school offer the athletic opportunities I'd want to participate in or cheer for? What will it mean to be an alumnus of the University of Miami rather than Miami University of Ohio?

You also need to look for the campus energy that matches your own. However, always be open to compromise. Your parents may have a differing opinion than you. If this is the case, you need to sit down with them and discuss the opportunities and options.

Keep yourself from procrastinating. You have some real serious thinking to do. Make a list of the good things and the bad to help you make your decision. Ask the opinions of friends and family members. Be sure to submit whatever is required to secure your spot in the freshman class before the given deadline. The admissions offer letter from the school usually lists what the exact requirements are as to your next steps.

If you have a tough time choosing between two or more schools, this is a positive sign. It means that you have done a good job in putting together your list. Whichever school you choose, chances are, you will be happy.

INTERNATIONAL COLLEGE COUNSELORS TIP:
Be sure to make the most of your college experience. Chances are, you'll never have the ability to return to a place with so many opportunities and so few responsibilities.

232

YOU ARE GOING TO COLLEGE!

Congratulations!

Once you have made your choice, accept it and rejoice. If you have followed the advice in this chapter, there is an excellent chance that your final college choice is the right one for you.

International students entering from outside the United States, make sure you obtain a student or exchange visitor visa. You need to apply for a U.S. visa at the nearest U.S. Embassy/Consulate. A visa is an endorsement on your passport indicating that you're allowed to enter the United States and stay for a specified period of time. I go into further detail about visas in the next chapter, but make sure to apply for your visa early to avoid possible delays. Check with the U.S. State Department for more details at

http://travel.state.gov

We wish you great success in your academic endeavors and hope that you enjoy your college studies. Remember, the college is accepting you—as a student. With the right credentials and the right application, you, too, can get into any school you choose!

Chapter 26

International Student Visas

To attend any college in the United States, international students need to complete certain paperwork to obtain a student visa.

When you are accepted by a U.S. school and your enrollment is confirmed, the school will enroll you in the Student and Exchange Visitor Information System (SEVIS). This will allow the school to issue you an I-20 or DS-2019 form, which you need in order to gain an F-1 or J-1 status. Either of these statuses will allow you to study in the United States, and either usually allows for on-campus and some off-campus work authorization. There are a few important differences between the two statuses, which are outlined below.

F-1 Status
All full-time degree-seeking students are eligible for the F-1 visa. It is the most common type used by international students in the United States, and most international students attending a college or university full-time have F-1 status.

J-1 Status
J-1 visa status is generally used for students in specific educational exchange programs, such as the Fulbright, LASPAU, DAAD, AmidEast, UC Education Abroad Program (EAP), or others. It may also be used by the university for students in certain degree programs. Know that the U.S. State Department requires specific health insurance coverage for J-1 students during their entire stay in the United States.

ELIGIBILITY

All students are eligible for an F-1 visa, as long as they have been admitted to a full-time program of study, meet the English language requirements, and can show proof of funding for at least the first year of study.

To be eligible for J-1 status, students must meet the following criteria:

▸ Have adequate financial support for all school and living expenses, including additional financial support for any accompanying family members, for the duration of the degree program.

and

▸ Have 51 percent of their total financial support coming from an institutional or government sponsor in the form of a scholarship, fellowship, assistantship, stipend, tuition waiver, or other direct support provided specifically for the educational program. Personal or family funds and loans or support from individuals do not qualify.

or

▸ Participate in a specific educational exchange program.

Main differences between F-1 and J-1 student visas

There are a few basic differences between the F-1 and J-1 visas:

	F-1 Status	J-1 Status
Source of Funding	Any student, funded either by personal or outside funds (or a combination of both) is eligible for F-1 status.	Must have at least 51 percent of total funding from a source other than personal family (or friends). Other than personal funds may include: a scholarship or a grant from an external funding source or a fellowship, assistantship in instruction (AI), or assistantship in research (AR). Other external funding sources may also include your home country government, an international organization, or a corporate sponsor.
Proof of Funding	To be eligible for F-1 visa, the newly admitted student must show the school and U.S. consulate proof of sufficient funding for his or her first year of study in the U.S.	To be eligible for J-1 visa, the newly admitted student must show the school and U.S. consulate proof of sufficient funding for the duration of his or her academic program in the U.S.

2-Year Home Country Residency Requirement	There is no home country residency requirement following the completion of program.	May be subject to a 2-year home country residency requirement if receiving government funding or if from the country from the Exchange Visitors Skills lists.
On Campus Employment	Limited to 20 hours per week while school is in session and available as full time during school vacation and holidays. On-campus employment is defined as work done on the premises of the school that issued the I-20.	Limited to 20 hours per week while school is in session, but can be full-time during official school breaks.
Health Insurance	Regulations do not require F-1 students and F-2 dependents to carry health insurance. However, some schools require every enrolled student to have health insurance coverage. For more information, please consult the university's health services website.	Federal law requires both J-1 students and their J-2 dependents to carry health insurance throughout the period of their stay. Insurance must meet the minimum defined by U.S. federal law.

NOTE: Students who study in J-1 student status for more than six months are barred from returning to the United States in a J-1 Research Scholar category (another J-1 visa category, often used for postdoctoral and other university research work) until 12 months after their program of studies in J-1 student status ends. An F-1 visa does not have this restriction.

APPLYING FOR A VISA

There are several steps to apply for an F-1 visa. The order of these steps and how you complete them may vary depending on the U.S. Embassy or Consulate where you apply. Make sure you consult the instructions available on the Embassy or Consulate website where you intend to apply.

In general, there are five stages when applying for a U.S. student F-1 visa:

1. Apply to and be accepted by a Student and Exchange Visitor Program (SEVP)–approved school in the United States (six to 12 months prior to U.S. study).

2. Pay the Student and Exchange Visitor Information System (SEVIS) fee.

3. Complete a U.S. student visa application along with recent photo(s).

4. Pay the visa application fee.

5. Schedule and attend a visa interview.

Read on for more detailed information on each of these five steps.

1. Apply to a SEVP-approved institution.

Before you can apply at a U.S. Embassy or Consulate for an F-1 student visa, you must first apply to and be accepted by a Student and Exchange Visitor Program (SEVP)–approved school. Visit the Homeland Security Study on the United States search page to confirm whether the colleges you are applying to or attending are SEVP-certified schools.

The website is https://studyinthestates.dhs.gov/school-search.

Accreditation is important, as it ensures that your college degree is recognized by other universities, professional associations, employers, and government ministries worldwide.

When you are accepted by the U.S. school you plan to attend, you will be enrolled in the Student and Exchange Visitor Information System (SEVIS). The U.S. school will provide you with a Form I-20 to present to the consular officer when you attend your visa interview. Visit the U.S. Immigration and Customs Enforcement (ICE) Student and Exchange Visitor Program (SEVP) website to learn more about SEVIS and the SEVIS I-901 fee.

The website is https://www.ice.gov/sevis.

2. Pay the I-901 SEVIS fee.
You must pay the I-901 SEVIS fee at least three days prior to submitting an application for a U.S. visa. In order to pay the fee, you need to file either an online or a paper form. Both can be accessed through the U.S. Immigration and Customs Enforcement (ICE) SEVP website.

The website is https://www.ice.gov/sevis/i901.

This website offers a narrated tutorial that walks you through the steps of paying the I-901 SEVIS fee.

Take care to follow the detailed requirements exactly as they appear on your I-20 or DS-2019 form.

At the time of publishing, the I-901 SEVIS fee is US $200 for F visa holders. The website explains the procedure for paying the fee by payment in U.S. dollars by credit card on fmjfee.com, or by check, money order, or bank draft.

Print a payment confirmation from the website after processing your payment. You need this confirmation as proof of fee payment at your U.S. student visa interview. You may also be required to show the confirmation to the customs officer at your chosen U.S. port of entry, if you change your nonimmigrant status, or if you apply for any other U.S. immigration benefits.

For I-901 SEVIS fee assistance:

▸ Email address: fmjfee.SEVIS@ice.dhs.gov

▸ I-901 SEVIS fee customer service hotline at 703-603-3400

3. Complete the online student visa application.
Once you have received your SEVIS form and paid the I-901 SEVIS fee, you can make an appointment with a U.S. Consulate or Embassy in your country for a U.S. student visa application. It's best to apply as early as possible, as visa processing times vary. Your visa can be issued up to 120 days before you're due to enter the United States.

All international students seeking visas need to complete the Online Nonimmigrant Visa Application Form DS-160 which can be found at https://ceac.state.gov/genniv/. You must complete the online visa application and print the application form confirmation page to take to your interview.

You will need to upload your photo while completing the online Form DS-160. Your photo must be in the format explained in the photograph requirements. If you are unable to upload the photo, you must bring one printed photo in the format explained in the photograph requirements. The photo should be printed on photo-quality paper

Most countries have their own dedicated website for everything necessary for getting a U.S. student visa. These pages can be accessed from https://ais.usvisa-info.com.

If your country is not on the list, you may find the U.S. Embassy or consulate in your country by using the U.S. Embassy website: http://www.usembassy.gov.

Select the location from which you are applying and ensure you have all the documents and information you need to fill in the application. After selecting and answering a security question, you'll be taken to the form. At the top you'll find your Application ID. Write this down. You will need this ID later to retrieve your form if you need to exit the application and return to it later.

Personal details required to complete the DS-160 form include:

▸ Name and date of birth

▸ Address and phone number

▸ Your National Identification Number, Taxpayer ID number, or Social Security identification number

▸ Passport details

▸ Details of travel plans and travel companions

▸ Details of any previous U.S. travel

▸ Your point of contact in the United States

▸ Family, work, and education details

▸ Security, background, and medical/health information

▸ Additional point of contact information (at least two contacts in your country of residence who can verify the info provided in your application)

▸ SEVIS ID and address of US school/program in which you intend to enroll

Make sure to answer all of the questions accurately and fully or you may have to reschedule your visa interview appointment.

Once the visa application form is completed, electronically sign your form by clicking the Sign Application button at the end. After your application is uploaded, you'll be sent a confirmation page with a barcode, barcode number, and your application ID number. Print this page and take it to your visa interview appointment.

4. Pay the visa application fee.
The visa application fee is also called the Machine Readable Visa Fee, or MRV fee. Make sure to review the fee payment instructions. In general, there are three ways to pay the non-refundable, non-transferable visa application fee:

▸   In person at an approved bank

▸   By phone (you'll receive a fee confirmation number)

▸   Online (you'll need to print your receipt)

The visa fee page offers the visa fee in U.S. dollars and local currency.

Print the receipt when you have finished paying. You may be asked for this fee receipt when you get to your visa interview appointment.

5. Schedule and attend a U.S. student visa interview.
You must schedule an appointment for your visa interview, generally, at the U.S. Embassy or Consulate in the country where you live. You may schedule your interview at any U.S. Embassy or Consulate, but be aware that it may be difficult to qualify for a visa outside of your place of permanent residence.

Appointments can be scheduled online or via phone, by calling your nearest U.S. Embassy or Consulate. Do not worry if you need to schedule your interview appointment at a different U.S. Embassy or Consulate other than the one you used to apply for your visa. The barcode from your DS-160 can be used to retrieve your information in any U.S. Embassy or Consulate.

Complete the visa fee payment first, as you may need to provide your visa fee number.

On the U.S. State Department website, you can check the estimated wait time for a visa interview appointment at a U.S. Embassy or Consulate: https://travel.state.gov/content/visas/en.html.

Documents Required for the Visa Interview
INTERNATIONAL COLLEGE COUNSELORS TIP:
Check the website of the Embassy or Consulate where you will apply to make sure you have all the required documents needed for your interview.

These documents include:

▸ Passport valid for at least six months beyond your period of stay in the United States (unless exempt by country-specific agreements). If more than one person is included in your passport, each person who needs a visa must submit a separate application.

▸ Both the SEVIS I-901 fee payment receipt and the visa application payment receipt, if you are required to pay before your interview.

▸ Photo. You will upload your photo while completing the online Form DS-160. As we said earlier in this chapter, if you are unable to upload the photo, you must bring one printed photo in the format explained in the photograph requirements. The photo should be printed on photo-quality paper.

▸ Certificate of Eligibility for Nonimmigrant (F-1) Student Status For Academic and Language Students, Form I-20. Your school will send you a SEVIS-generated Form I-20 once they have entered your information in the SEVIS database. You and your school official must sign the Form I-20. All students must be registered in SEVIS (the Student and Exchange Visitor System).

Additional Documentation May Be Required
Review the instructions for how to apply for a visa on the website of the Embassy or consulate where you will apply: http://www.usembassy.gov/.

Additional documents may be requested to establish that you are qualified. For example:

▸ Transcripts, diplomas, degrees, or certificates from previous schools you attended. Bring along a separate written list of all of your previous employers and schools you have attended for reference.

▸ Standardized test scores required by your U.S. school, such as scores from the TOEFL, SAT, ACT, etc.

▸ Your declaration of intent to depart the United States upon completion of your course of study.

▸ Financial evidence showing that you or your sponsor (i.e., parents or a government sponsor) has sufficient funds to cover your tuition, travel, and living expenses during your stay in the United States.

▸ DS-160 application confirmation page with barcode and application ID number.

▸ Printed copy of visa interview appointment letter.

Attending the Visa Interview

Be early for your visa interview. This is very important. If you are late, you may be asked to reschedule for another day. In most cases only applicants with a scheduled appointment will be allowed inside the Embassy or Consulate. Exceptions include a parent for children under the age of 18, translators, and assistants for the disabled. If you need to bring a parent, translator, or assistant, contact the Embassy or Consulate right after scheduling your interview to give them the name of the person who will accompany you.

The purpose of the visa interview is for the consular officer to determine whether you are qualified to receive a U.S. student visa and, if so, which visa category is appropriate for you.

Examples of F-1 Visa Interview Questions

- Why did you choose to study in the United States instead of joining the workforce in your home country?

- Why did you choose this school, and why is it the best school for you?

- What are your test scores (SAT, ACT, TOEFL), your GPA, and your overall performance as a student in the past?

- How are you funding the entire duration of your education, including tuition, room and board, transportation, and all other expenses?

- After you graduate, will you return home, or will you stay in the United States?

Ink-free, digital fingerprint scans will be taken as part of your application process. This usually happens at your visa interview.

After your interview, the consular officer will tell you whether your application requires further administrative processing. This usually means that more time will pass before you receive your visa. Wait times vary depending on the country.

When the visa is approved, you may pay a visa issuance fee depending on your nationality. You will also be informed as to how your passport with the visa will be returned to you. Review the visa processing time to learn how soon your passport with your visa will be ready for pickup or delivery by the courier.

F-1 visas can be issued up to 120 days in advance of your study start date, but you will not be allowed to enter the United States any earlier than thirty days before your start date. J-1 visas can be issued at any time. If you want to enter the United States before the thirty-day period, you must qualify for and obtain a visitor visa. The 30-day policy does not apply to students who are continuing their studies. Continuing students may enter the United States at any time before their classes start. Continuing students may also renew their visas at any time, as long as they have maintained student status and their SEVIS records are current.

INTERNATIONAL COLLEGE COUNSELORS TIP:
As there is no guarantee you will be issued a visa, do not make final travel plans or buy airline tickets until you have secured a visa.

Maintaining Your F-1 Status

F-1 status covers the period of time when you are a full-time registered student making normal progress toward your degree (or exchange program). It can also cover an optional period of practical training following the completion of your studies. Plus, you have a 60-day period of time called a "grace period" to prepare to depart the United States or change to another status.

As an F-1 student, you must meet certain obligations in order to maintain legal immigration status. Maintaining this status is necessary in order to receive the benefits of F-1 status and it can be crucial to a successful application for a change or adjustment of visa status in the future. Failure to maintain your non-immigrant status can result in serious problems with immigration and could lead to deportation from the United States.

To maintain lawful status, an F-1 student must:

▸ Attend any mandatory immigration check-in programs.

▸ Attend the university they are authorized to attend.

▸ Complete immigration school transfer procedures when necessary.

▸ Be in good academic standing and make progress in an academic program.

▸ Extend their I-20 prior to its expiration date if they are unable to complete their academic program by the original expiration date.

▸ In the event of change of academic program or level, update their

I-20 in a timely fashion in accordance with immigration regulations.

- Maintain full-time enrollment during the academic year.

- Undergraduate students must enroll in 12 credit hours per term while graduate students must enroll in 8 credit hours (or number of credit hours defined by the specific graduate program) per term. Courses taken for "audit" or "visit" do not count toward the full-time enrollment requirement for immigration purposes.

- Suspension, dismissal, enrollment withheld, expulsion, or any other similar action that prevents enrollment may have an effect on legal immigration status.

- Limit on-campus employment to 20 hours per week during academic year.

- Reject unauthorized employment and refrain from working off campus without authorization.

- Keep a valid passport at all times. The passport must be valid for at least six months ahead on the day they return to the United States from a trip abroad.

- Maintain health insurance coverage.

- Complete any departure forms if leaving a program before the end date of the I-20.

- Update current and permanent address information with a school in a timely manner.

- Meet any other requirements of the school or program.

How to Apply for a U.S. Student J-1 Visa
There are several steps to apply for a J-1 visa.

1. Find a J-1 Sponsor.
To apply for a J-1 visa, you need a designated sponsor to accept you into their program. The United States State Department has an official

list of designated sponsor organizations in the United States. Note that sponsoring organizations can help you with applying for a J-1 visa. Students can find these designated sponsor organizations at http://j1visa.state.gov/participants/.

2. Apply for the DS-2019.

Once you have applied to and been approved by a designated sponsor organization, the next step is to submit the DS-2019 Form, also known as the Certificate of Eligibility for Exchange Visitor (J-1) Status. This form will permit you to schedule an interview with the U.S. Embassy or Consulate. This form is issued by your designated sponsoring organization and will include a description of the exchange visitors' program, including the start and end date, category of exchange, and an estimate of the cost of the exchange program. The information in this form is completed by the sponsor before being given to the participant. Once you have the DS-2019, you can apply at a U.S. Embassy or Consulate for the J-1 visa.

3. Pay the I-901 SEVIS fee.

You will be required to pay a I-901 SEVIS fee as part of your J-1 visa application. Before you pay, first check to see whether this fee was already part of your program fees to your sponsoring organization. Your sponsor can tell you if this fee will be paid by you, or for you by your sponsor. If the sponsor pays your I-901 SEVIS fee, be sure to get a receipt confirming payment.

At the time of publishing, the I-901 SEVIS fee for a J-1 visa is US $180.

For I-901 SEVIS fee assistance:

- Email address: fmjfee.SEVIS@ice.dhs.gov
- I-901 SEVIS fee customer service hotline at +1 703 603-3400

4. Pay the Nonimmigrant Visa Application Processing Fee.

The Nonimmigrant Visa Application Processing Fee is currently US $160 and can be paid by visiting the State Department's Fee for Visa

Services. If you are participating in a program with the U.S. Government, State Department, U.S. Agency for International Development (USAID), or a U.S. Government–funded educational and cultural exchange program, you do not have to pay this fee as part of your J-1 visa application.

5. Schedule and attend a U.S. student visa interview.

You must schedule an appointment for your visa interview, generally at the U.S. Embassy or Consulate in the country where you live. You may schedule your interview at any U.S. Embassy or Consulate, but be aware that it may be difficult to qualify for a visa outside of your home country.

Schedule an appointment online or via phone by calling the nearest U.S. Embassy or Consulate. Do not worry if you need to schedule your interview appointment at a different U.S. Embassy or Consulate than the one you used to apply for your visa. The barcode from your DS-160 can be used to retrieve your information in any U.S. Embassy or Consulate.

Complete the visa fee payment first, as you may need to provide your visa fee number.

On the U.S. State Department website, you can check the estimated wait-time for a visa interview appointment at a U.S. Embassy or Consulate: https://travel.state.gov/content/visas/en.html.

Documents Required for the Visa Interview

Check the website of the Embassy or Consulate where you will apply to make sure you have all the required documents needed for your interview.

These documents include:

- Passport valid for at least six months beyond your period of stay in the United States (unless exempt by country-specific agreements).

▸ Form DS-2019: Certificate of Eligibility for Exchange Visitor Status. Your program sponsor will give you and any family members traveling with you a SEVIS-generated Form 2019, which you will be required to bring with you for the J-1 visa interview.

▸ Both the I-901 SEVIS fee payment receipt and the visa application payment receipt, if you are required to pay before your interview.

▸ Photo. You will upload your photo while completing the online Form DS-160. If you are unable to upload the photo, you must bring one printed photo in the format explained in the photograph requirements. The photo should be printed on photo-quality paper.

▸ Form DS-7002 (for J-1 Trainee and Intern visa applicants only).

Additional Documentation May Be Required
Review the instructions for how to apply for a visa on the website of the U.S. Embassy or Consulate where you will apply at http://www.usembassy.gov/.

Additional documents may be requested to establish that you are qualified. For example:

▸ Transcripts, diplomas, degrees, or certificates from previous schools you attended. Bring along a separate written list of all your previous employers and schools you have attended for reference.

▸ Standardized test scores required by your U.S. school, such as the TOEFL, SAT, ACT, etc.

▸ Your declaration of intent to depart the United States upon completion of the course of study.

▸ Financial evidence showing that you or your sponsor (i.e., your parents or a government sponsor) has sufficient funds to cover your tuition, travel, and living expenses during your stay in the United States.

▸ DS-160 application confirmation page with barcode and

application ID number.

▸ Printed copy of visa interview appointment letter.

Attending the Visa Interview

Be early for your visa interview. This is very important. If you are late, you may be asked to reschedule for another day. In most cases, only applicants with a scheduled appointment will be allowed inside the Embassy or Consulate. Exceptions include a parent for people under the age of 18, translators, and assistants for the disabled. If you need to bring a parent, translator, or assistant, contact your chosen Embassy or Consulate right after scheduling your interview to give them the name of the person who will accompany you.

The purpose of the visa interview is for the consular officer to determine whether or not you are qualified to receive a U.S. student visa and, if so, which visa category is appropriate for you.

Examples of J-1 Visa Interview Questions

▸ Why do you want to go to the United States?

▸ What are your qualifications?

▸ What are you currently doing?

▸ Which university are you enrolled at (or, have you graduated from)?

▸ To what program are you applying?

▸ When did you apply for this program?

▸ How much was your placement fee?

▸ Who is going to pay for your expenses? How much do you/they make?

▸ Tell me about your housing situation.

▸ What will you be doing in the United States?

251

Ink-free, digital fingerprint scans will be taken as part of your application process. This usually happens at your visa interview.

After your interview, the consular officer will tell you whether your application requires further administrative processing. This usually means that more time will pass before you receive your visa. Wait times vary depending on country.

When the visa is approved, you may pay a visa issuance fee depending on your nationality. You will also be informed how your passport with your visa will be returned to you. Review the visa processing time to learn how soon your passport with your visa will be ready for pickup or delivery by the courier.

When You Arrive to the United States
Federal law requires you to carry "registration" documents at all times, including your I-20 and your passport with I-94 card attached or admission stamp. (More on these later in the chapter.)

Always carry your passport and visa-related documents in your hand luggage. When you arrive in the United States, you will need to have the following items available to present at the immigration inspection point:

- A valid passport (passports should be valid for at least six months into the future)

- A valid U.S. visa (Canadians do not require a visa)

- An immigration document (an I-20 for F-1 status or a DS-2019 for J-1 status)

- A receipt for the SEVIS I-901 fee

- Evidence of funding

In airports, immigration inspection is located before the baggage collection—so keep these items in your hand luggage so that you can easily access them.

For day-to-day purposes, keep these documents in a secure location such as a bank safe-deposit box, and carry photocopies with you. However, if you are traveling outside of the area of your school, you should carry the original documents with you. If you are traveling by air, train, bus, or ship, you may be required to produce these documents before boarding. Keep photocopies of all your documents in a separate location in case your documents are lost or stolen.

I-94 Arrival and Departure Record

When you enter the United States, you are issued either an admission stamp in your passport or Form I-94, a small white card usually stapled inside your passport by an immigration official at the U.S. port of entry. These are proof of your legal entry into the United States. The I-94 is also called the Arrival-Departure Record.

For most travelers arriving by air or sea, a paper I-94 card will not be issued. Instead, the Customs and Border Protection (CBP) official will issue an admission stamp in your passport. Travelers at land borders currently receive paper I-94 cards.

The admission stamp or I-94 card records the date and place that you entered the United States, your immigration status (for example, F-1 or J-1), and your authorized period of stay (indicated by "D/S," meaning "duration of status"). Both of these are important records. They show that you have been legally admitted to the United States, the class of your admission, and your authorized period of stay.

You can legally stay in the United States for the duration of your status, which means the time needed for your college program to be completed.

Be sure to check the stamp to make sure it is correct. If you receive a paper I-94 card, keep it stapled in your passport. A US $330 fee is required to replace a lost, stolen, or damaged paper I-94 card. Consult your international student advisor if you lose your I-94 card.

You might also need a printout of your electronic I-94 information to apply for various benefits, such as state ID cards or a Social Security number. You can obtain a printout of your I-94 record at CBP.gov/I94.

Chapter 27

Calendars

At most high schools, college guidance does not begin until your final year of high school or the year before. And while this is "normal" and keeps college stress to a minimum, for those looking to attend a college in the U.S., I recommend that students start to think about college goals as early as their first year in high school, known in the United States as the freshman year of high school, or ninth grade. Of course, this book is a great place to start.

Below is a year-by-year checklist that will help keep you on track and avoid any last-minute scrambles.

HIGH SCHOOL FRESHMAN YEAR

Time Management
- Review your schedule at the beginning of the school year. The goal is to enroll in the most challenging classes you can handle.

- If possible, try to meet with a school counselor to discuss college plans. If you are considering hiring an independent counselor, make sure to find a company, such as International College Counselors, who will begin working with you in your freshman year and who has experience working with international students.

- Don't procrastinate.

- Keep a calendar. Update it regularly with any important dates and deadlines.

Standardized Tests
Familiarize yourself with the SAT Subject Tests. Take the tests as soon as you finish the higher-level courses your school offers (usually AP or IB) so the material is still fresh in your mind. While taking the highest-level courses your school offers is rarely the case for freshmen, it can happen. Subject Tests for freshmen may include World History,

Biology E/M, and Chemistry.

Read! It's the best way to prepare for the SAT, ACT, and all other standardized exams.

Extracurricular Activities
Get involved with extracurricular activities. Find something you know you enjoy or have an interest in. This way, chances are you'll stick with it over the next four years. Colleges like to see that you stay with something and then move up in it. Cooking, choir, Model United Nations, student government, cycling, ceramics, speech and debate, or starting a business—it's all good. Many extracurricular activities show initiative, organizational skills, critical thinking, imagination, creativity, responsibility, commitment, and teamwork. Explore interests outside the school, as well.

Key Projects or Involvement
Want to create something meaningful that will stand out for your college applications? Whether you're starting a mentorship program, a public safety campaign, a new program or class, a nonprofit, or a business venture, your freshman year is a great time to get started.

Money
Talk with your parents about financing college. Talking about money will help you understand how much college really costs, and how you can help defray the costs through applying for private scholarships, taking AP courses, IB courses, or British A-Levels, and getting good grades.

Learning Differences
If you think you have a learning difference, be sure to get tested as soon as possible. You'll want to start getting the accommodations you may need to succeed.

Summer
It's never too early to start with meaningful summer opportunities. Do some networking, and ask your parents and your friends' parents to

help you network, too. If you're interested in accounting, see who is in your network that you might be able to call. The same goes for if you want to be a graphic designer or a veterinarian. Many businesses wouldn't mind a free volunteer.

Search online for summer programs for high school students at colleges, if this is the route you choose. Remember there is no "right" way to spend a summer—and you get no extra points for attending expensive, faraway programs. The key is to engage in activities that are meaningful to you and that provide opportunities for personal growth.

Learning about Colleges

Start to explore college websites and talk to friends who studied in the United States about colleges they're attending. Visit college campuses if you can. At this point in the game, it's low pressure. If your family takes a vacation in the United States, make it a point to visit college campuses near your destination. Even if the schools are not on your radar, these visits will give everyone a chance to get a feel for the options that are available.

HIGH SCHOOL SOPHOMORE

Time Management

- Review your schedule at the beginning of the school year. Continue to revise your academic program. The goal is to enroll in challenging classes that will help you prepare for college without overwhelming you.

- Keep up with your calendar. Update it regularly with any important dates and deadlines.

Standardized Tests

- Try to take the PSAT, which is given in October. Several international locations offer this to students starting in the tenth grade. Take this test for practice.

- If relevant, register for SAT Subject Tests in May or June. Take SAT Subject Tests and other tests like AP exams as appropriate.

- Keep reading!

Extracurricular Activities

Stay involved in extracurricular activities. It's not too late to try new activities if you don't like the ones you participated in last year. Find something you know you will enjoy or have an interest in.

Revisit key activities and see how you can expand on your interests and abilities. Like volleyball? Consider starting a volleyball program for low-income students. Find that you are good at math? Enter national math competitions. Now is the time to start differentiating yourself, and exploring your academic path.

Money

Keep talking with your parents about financing college. How much are they able and willing to contribute to your education? Has their financial situation changed since your last conversation?

Surf the Internet for scholarship opportunities for sophomores. Apply for as many scholarships as possible. Make sure to meet all deadlines to apply.

Summer

- Plan to do something exciting and explore a major interest. Interested in science or math? Consider one of the many competitive science/math summer programs, such as MIT's Research Science Institute (RSI) or Boston University's Program in Mathematics for Young Scientists.

- Start visiting a few colleges.

- Use the summer to study for the SAT or ACT.

HIGH SCHOOL JUNIOR

Junior year is the homestretch. The critical decisions that are made this year could have a major impact on the next five years of your life—and far beyond. This is the year when students start narrowing their lists of colleges and potential academic paths. This is the last full year of grades that college admissions officers will review.

Don't let the college admissions process feel so overwhelming that you become frozen, missing deadlines and forgetting important details. Read this book and follow its instructions, and you'll be fine.

Time Management

▸ Review your schedule at the beginning of the school year. You want to enroll in challenging classes that will help you prepare for college. If you are aiming for the most competitive schools, you must take the most rigorous curriculum offered by your school. Care must be taken not to overload on classes or extracurricular activities, however, as junior year courses and grades are critical. But you also need to show the college admissions team that you can push yourself. Academically, this rule about focusing on grades and curriculum is relevant at all colleges—from the Ivy League to the less competitive schools.

▸ If you have not already done so, and you have one, get to know your college counselor. They will likely be writing a letter of recommendation on your behalf. They can also make you aware of key scholarships and school awards.

▸ For those working with an independent counselor, set up a schedule for working together. This is an important year for their support.

▸ Keep a calendar. Update it regularly with any important dates and deadlines.

Standardized Tests

- Try to take the PSAT, which is typically given in October.

- As soon as possible, plan your junior year testing schedule. You can take either the SAT or up to three SAT Subject Tests on one test day, or the ACT, which is offered on other dates. You should aim to take the SAT and the ACT tests before the end of your junior year. As previously mentioned, we always recommend that students try both the SAT and the ACT. The colleges (Ivies included) accept them equally, and students often have a natural inclination toward one test.

- Take AP/IB examinations.

- Take the TOEFL or IELTS.

Extracurricular Activities

Colleges want to see that a student sticks with something. Remain involved with your extracurricular activities. This year is very important. If you can, assume leadership roles in extracurricular activities. Now is the year to showcase your abilities at regional, national, or international competitions. Colleges aren't looking for quantity in activities, but quality and advancement. This is your last year for colleges to understand your strength in debate, robotics, or art (to name a few subjects). Don't be ashamed to seek out opportunities to compete and shine.

Similarly, service activities should also receive focus this year. Remember, the key to service is for the activity to be meaningful and impactful. It's not about how much money you raise or how far you travel to perform your service. Some of the best service activities can be found in your own city and require little more than dedication, time, and creativity.

College Selection/Application Preparation

- Get to know the junior year teachers—and leave a positive impression on them. This is preparation for those all-important college recommendations.

- Start narrowing down colleges and universities. Information can be gathered in books and on websites. Try to talk to alumni or current students. In the spring, draft an initial college list. Before the start of your senior year, the goal is to develop a list of 15 to 20 colleges of interest.

- Talk about your career choice(s). These may have a big impact on the list of potential colleges to be considered. The idea here is not to commit to a career path, but to try to narrow down the career possibilities.

- Go on college campus tours—as many as possible. Try to look at the whole range of schools: public, private, large, and small. Consider taking a college road tour over spring break.

- Attend any college fairs that come to your area, as well as any presentations by traveling college admissions officers.

Money

- Keep talking with your parents about financing for college. Make sure your parents' financial situation or the amount they can contribute has not changed since your previous conversation.

- Research scholarship opportunities for juniors and apply for them. Make sure to proofread everything on your applications and meet all deadlines.

Summer

- Find a meaningful summer opportunity. This could include an internship, a job, or a college program. Whatever it is, start early. You want to beat the competition.

- This is the year when many competitive and prestigious summer programs are available. Interested in engineering? Journalism? Business? Consider filling out a few applications for programs that will help you learn and also look great on your college applications. Also consider summer programs at a college of interest. While this does not guarantee admission, it will help you to confirm your interest in the school and may make your early decision choices easier.

- Start to work on those college applications. Schools with rolling admissions will accept applications as early as August or September, and early applications could mean early acceptance. For those schools not accepting applications until November or January, I still recommend that you complete your applications and essays in the summer. There are no downsides to starting early, and many international students do not apply early so it will make you stand out. Additionally, it will save you significant time in the always-busy fall months.

- If you plan to retake your SAT, ACT, TOEFL, or IELTS in the fall, study as much as you can. This is your last chance!

All Year 'Round
Read! It's the best way to prepare for all standardized exams.

HIGH SCHOOL SENIOR

For seniors, we've broken the "to-do" list down by months since there is a lot more to do in this year.

August/September
- Confirm your college target list, and consider Early Action, Early Decision, and rolling admission possibilities.

- Plan to retake the SAT, ACT, TOEFL, or IELTS as needed.

- Continue working on key target applications.

- Assign your recommenders/get your recommendation forms to your teachers and counselors early.

- Discuss with your high school counselor the colleges to which you want to apply, and establish deadlines for the mailing of your transcripts. Remember that transcripts must be in English, so give yourself time to get them translated by a certified company.

October

- Do well academically—strong grades can have a major impact for regular admissions and if you are deferred from Early Decision.

- Complete Early Decision applications. Don't forget to send your test scores, transcripts, and any letters of recommendation.

- Get all necessary financial aid forms together and explore scholarship opportunities.

- Ask your bank for a statement or certification of finances, which is usually requested with the application or once students are admitted. Confirm which financial forms are needed for each of your colleges.

- Check web portals/email for any communication from colleges.

November

- Early Decision/Action candidates should be sure not to miss the application deadline this month.

- Arrange interviews with alumni and admissions representatives of colleges where interviews are available over the next several months.

- Send updates to schools to which you applied early. Include in those updates any new activities or awards received since your application submission.

- Check web portals/email for any communication from colleges.

December

- This is likely your last chance to take the ACT, SAT, SAT Subject Tests, TOEFL, and IELTS for fall admissions.

- If not on the Common Application, give your counselor, principal, or designated school official the secondary school report section of your college application forms early this month.

- If you have not done so already, give recommendation

links/forms for each college to appropriate teachers and others. Let the teachers/counselors know if the Common Application will be emailing them directly.

▸ Be sure to continue working with your parents on appropriate financial aid forms. Early Decision applicants who have been admitted must withdraw any other applications.

▸ Early Decision applicants who have been deferred or rejected and non-Early Decision Round I applicants should consider Early Decision Round II opportunities at their first-choice school, if they have one and are ready to make a binding commitment.

▸ Preferably all applications should be completed and sent out prior to holiday vacation.

January

▸ Applications for admission and financial aid forms must be mailed out or filed electronically to meet deadlines. Make copies of everything and check all details before submitting.

▸ Make sure recommendations and transcripts are being mailed/emailed.

▸ If you have been deferred from an Early Decision or Early Action school, do not dismay! Start writing a letter to the admissions office, bringing them up-to-date on your classes, activities, and continuing interest in the college. Send in any new materials or information worthy of inclusion in your application, for example, an additional recommendation from a senior-year teacher or new grades.

▸ Don't forget to keep up those grades. Good grades in the winter and spring can make a significant difference for deferred applications, regular applications, and, perhaps, a waiting list situation in May/June.

▸ Check web portals/email for any communication from colleges.

February

▸ Arrange now to take any final exams in May or June. Some, such as AP or IB exams, could save you time and money in college!

▸ This is a good month to do self-marketing with faculty members and coaches at colleges.

▸ Send updates to early schools, including new awards, honors, or accomplishments received since the application was submitted.

▸ Finish all college applications.

▸ Take advantage of any alumni interviews that a college may offer to you.

March

▸ This month you will receive your letters of admission.

▸ Check web portals/email for any communication from colleges.

▸ Clear up sources of financial aid. Don't forget to apply for scholarships!

▸ Continue to work hard academically, and keep colleges informed of your progress, extracurricular achievements, and other awards.

April

▸ Continue to check web portals/email for any communication from colleges.

▸ Visit one or more campuses if necessary to help decide which college to accept.

▸ Make sure you are getting the best possible financial aid package, and let the financial aid office know of any dissatisfaction or questions you have. Aid packages can be revised.

▸ If you still want to attend a college that has wait-listed you, let the admissions office know your desire—send admissions officers any new information, such as high grades or awards.

▸ Don't miss enrollment deposit deadlines.

- Send in your Statement or Certification of Finances if requested by the school and not required as part of the application.

- Complete and return the Entry Document Application Form, known as the I-20 (this is only given once you are accepted). The college will process and approve the I-20 form and mail the I-20 to you. You will then need to present this document to the U.S. consulate in your country of citizenship to receive your F-1 or J-1 student visa.

- Check web portals/email for any communication from colleges.

May
- Notification of acceptance deadline is May 1, known as the common reply date. You should also notify colleges you regretfully do not plan to attend, thanking them for accepting you.

- Take AP/IB examinations.

- Take SAT Subject Tests as appropriate. This might help you gain extra credits and advanced course placement in college. (Check with your school.)

- Research health insurance options for your time aboard.

June
- Respond promptly to all requests from your college regarding housing preferences and preliminary selection of courses for your first semester.

- Notify your high school to which college it should send your final grades, class ranking, and proof of graduation.

- Plan to earn money this summer, or to get a head start on any college courses you will be taking.

- Make plans for any pre-orientation or freshman trip programs at the college.

- Drop a note of appreciation to your high school counselor, independent counselor, teachers, and any others who have helped you in the admission process.

▸ Celebrate your high school success!

▸ Pass this book along to a sibling or friend. Let them know that while applying to college in the U.S. is hard, it is certainly not impossible.